HOW
TO BE
A MAN

HOW
TO BE
A MAN

(and other illusions)

Duff McKagan

DA CAPO PRESS
A Member of the Perseus Books Group

Parts of these stories and descriptions previously appeared on Seattle
Weekly.com, ESPN.com, and NFL.com.

Letter on pages 237–238 printed with permission of Chris Gehrt.

Designed by Linda Mark
Set in 12-point Fairfield LT Std Light by the Perseus Books Group

Library of Congress Cataloging-in-Publication Data
McKagan, Duff.
  How to be a man : (and other illusions) / Duff McKagan, with Chris
Kornelis.
    pages cm
  Includes bibliographical references and index.
  ISBN 978-0-306-82387-9 (hardcover)—
  ISBN 978-0-306-82388-6 (e-book) 1. McKagan, Duff. 2. Rock
musicians—United States—Biography. 3. Bass guitarists—United
States—Biography. I. Kornelis, Chris. II. Title.
  ML419.M352A3 2015
  787.87'166092—dc22
  [B]

                                                    2015002850

Published by Da Capo Press
A Member of the Perseus Books Group
www.dacapopress.com

Da Capo Press books are available at special discounts for bulk
purchases in the U.S. by corporations, institutions, and other orga-
nizations. For more information, please contact the Special Markets
Department at the Perseus Books Group, 2300 Chestnut Street,
Suite 200, Philadelphia, PA 19103, or call (800) 810-4145,
ext. 5000, or e-mail special.markets@perseusbooks.com.

10 9 8 7 6 5 4 3 2

For the women who have made me a better man
Susan, Grace, and Mae

CONTENTS

START WITH A STRONG BASE

I didn't wear my thong, but I brought plenty of oils and creams.

As part of my preparation for a tour of South America with Kings of Chaos, my wife, Susan, helped me pack my bag and pointed me toward our local tanning salon.

If I am good at anything at all, it is the complicated dance of international travel. After more than three decades on the road and in the sky, I've seen it all. Engines have fallen out of planes I've been in. Wars have broken out, and hurricanes have hit regions I've been traveling to. At this point in my life—just a few short months before my fiftieth birthday—I know how to take care of myself. I know what shots to get for malaria. I know how to prevent really bad jet lag. And I know how to avoid getting burned in the Southern Hemisphere.

To start, you've gotta get a little base tan going before you head down. Our winter is their summer, and you can get completely roasted onstage when the sun sets on your face if you've got nothing more than a Seattle tan. I know firsthand how hard it is to play through a burn to my face, chest, and arms. And I've seen friends go through much worse: I once saw the alabaster Melissa Auf de Maur suffer second-degree burns and have to be carted away in ice by paramedics.

I went in. I applied the cream. I rubbed in some oils. I listened to sports radio. I got brown.

When I went back to the counter, the dude-ish fella stopped me by name. "I heard you on the Jim Rome show." There were tears in his eyes.

I don't remember the '80s. I remember being in a band. I remember my family. I remember the friends I lost to addiction. I am fully aware that I am lucky to have emerged. But I have no cultural touchstones to speak of. I never saw *Cheers*. I didn't go to the movies. I didn't have any meaningful relationships with women, although I romanticized romance itself. My skin peeled away from my hands and feet. My nose bled. My kidneys hurt when I pissed. I woke up thirsty. I drank vodka.

When I finally got sober, I grabbed on to anything I could that would fill an hour, half hour, minute, or moment of not drinking and drugging. I read books on the Civil War. I devoured Ernest Hemingway. I bought VHS tapes on history: *Roots,* Ken Burns's *The Civil War,* Oliver Stone's *JFK*—anything that would keep my mind off the gnawing monster in my head that was trying to convince me that I needed narcotic relief. I learned to play golf because it took up five whole hours of a day. I rode my mountain bike. I became ravenous in my quest for martial arts knowledge and conditioning.

For the first time in my life, I was getting up at seven and going to bed at a decent hour. I was trying to find out what normal people did during the day.

The minute I got sober, I realized I had to get rid of my little black address book. It was full of names and numbers of people that I either drank heavily with or who supplied me with drugs. When I was in the thick of it, I had no shortage of companionship. Once I was sober, I realized I had no teetotaling friends.

Golf, reading, and hitting the dojo are all well and good, but I quickly realized that a man needs someone to talk to—some intellectual discourse.

A friend told me about an AM sports radio talk show host named Jim Rome. He hosted a new show that aired primarily in Southern California. He used "Welcome to the Jungle" as his intro music, and I started listening to make sure it wasn't some bullshit show. (As an artist, you want your songs to be heard in the right light, or said songs may be seen in a negative way afterward.)

At first, I wasn't quite sure how to take Jim's harsh slant on sports. He was brash, and his jokes and references all seemed directed toward regular listeners. But I followed up the next day. And the next. By the end of the first week, I got some of the inside jokes Jim Rome was on about. I discovered that us Rome listeners were dubbed the "Clones." When the weekend came, I missed my time with Jim Rome between nine and noon. I looked forward to Monday.

I got myself a ridiculous AM radio headset with the antenna rising high above the right ear speaker. The only set I could find was, of course, bright yellow. I didn't give a shit. Now I could listen to Rome while I was riding my mountain bike or running or playing golf. I made sure I went to the dojo before or after "The Jungle." I found that if I could just listen one more day to his show, it would be another day sober. Jim Rome helped keep me on the wagon.

As the months became years, I kept my ear tuned to Jim's show as it became widely syndicated and blew up nationally. I was always proud to be a Clone.

My sports knowledge grew through the show. Jim Rome always seemed to be the smartest guy in the room. But the thing about him is that he doesn't suffer fools lightly. When callers aren't clear and concise, Jim takes their heads off. As a listener, it's pure entertainment to laugh at the poor suckers that get pummeled by Romey. I was pretty goddamn sure I would never, ever, be one of those poor souls.

Until 2012, when I was promoting my first book, *It's So Easy (and other lies)*.

I undertook a pretty meaty promotional campaign. I did *Dr. Phil*, the BBC's *HARDtalk*, and whatever CNN was calling its morning show at the time. Then I got the call that Jim Rome wanted me to be a guest on his show. Oh, shit. What if he tears me a new one? What if he throws me under the bus for being a bad writer or too full of myself or having bad posture and a crappy first name and teenage acne? What if he does to me what I'd heard him do to so many guests on his show who didn't rise to the occasion?

But I promised myself at the beginning of 2012 that I'd say yes to things I'd previously said no to. This was the year to get over some fears that I hadn't attended to in my sober life. OK, what the hell? I'd go on *The Jim Rome Show*.

I don't really remember what happened on the show. I know that he kept me on for a really long time. I told him that his show had kept me sober and that without it I may not have survived. I told him that things had gotten so bad that I would drink my throwup for the alcohol in it. I explained that I was better now and had a wife and two really great girls and that I love the Seattle Seahawks.

He didn't tear me a new one, even after I was sure I blew it. He thanked me for the call, and that was it. I had a really great week in book sales afterward, and people on the street came up to me to thank me for what I'd said on the show. For my part, I was still in a bit of shock. I hate the sound of my own voice, so I don't go back and listen to interviews. To this day, I don't really know—nor do I want to know—what happened on the show. I'm just glad I made it out alive.

At the tanning salon, the dude behind the counter told me that the day he heard me on Jim Rome he was struggling with opiates and strung out in a big way. He went into rehab the same day, and if he hadn't heard the show, he told me, he may not have made it. Sixteen months sober, he was in a program. As tears filled his eyes, I felt mine well up too.

Jim Rome saved us both.

This life is crazy. It's the little things that can be absolute game changers. This guy in the tanning salon hugged me before I left, and I now have a deep bond with an absolute stranger. That bond is much deeper than anything I had with the people—my best friends—that were in my little black address book that I threw out into the rubbish bin of my darkest years.

MIND YOUR BUSINESS

Like the people you work with. Or at least use the animosity within your band, office, or team as a springboard for great fucking art (or commerce).

Have a kick-ass name. Unless your crew is so good that your name is THAT secondary, choose a name that means something and has some sort of imagery that is a reflection of what you do.

Watch how the business works around you. Ask questions constantly, and never be embarrassed to do so. "How much does a T-shirt cost to make?" or "What does publishing really mean?"

From the start, try to ascertain that you and your colleagues have the same goals. Back when Guns N' Roses first started, there *was* a different lead guitar player and drummer. When Axl, Izzy, and I booked a punk rock–style tour of the West Coast in 1985 and these two other guys didn't want to leave the comfort of LA, we went and found guys who DID! Thankfully and serendipitously, we found Slash and Steven Adler.

Be on time. Uh-huh.

Turn problems into opportunity. If your guitar breaks, jump into the crowd and say hello to your peeps. If your van goes tits up, become a better V-8 engine mechanic. If a promoter is being a dumb-dumb, make that a time for enlightening said prick to the better side of humanity. Walk away, and thank the gods of rock and roll that you are not a dick. And, really . . .

Don't be a dick. This is the most important step to having a positive experience in any business (especially rock and roll).

Don't climb up onto a speaker cabinet unless you are really going to jump. Have you ever seen that gig where the performer gets all the way up to the top of a cabinet and then realizes it is just too damn high? The awkward climb down is one of the most embarrassing moves in rock and roll (and every other profession).

Remember why you're there: You're doing what you love. You're feeding your family. Go kick some ass.

Shut it. Never miss an opportunity to keep your mouth shut. Whether you are talking to an audience, boring them with your banter, or regaling stories on the tour bus, don't talk too much.

Don't smoke crack on a leased private jet. Seriously, the smell gets into everything.

DON'T BURN ANY BRIDGES

A FEW DAYS AFTER MY MAN-TAN, I WAS ONSTAGE AT the Avalon Hollywood playing "Paradise City" with Kings of Chaos. Slash was to my left, Gilby Clarke to my right, and Matt Sorum was behind the drums. I've been through heaven and hell with these guys. But the character wrapped in scarves who wandered up onstage? I'd never seen him before.

Everyone was singing, having a good time. But I couldn't understand why a stranger had just joined the band. I nudged my bass tech, McBob. "Who's the guy with the scarves? Get him out of here!" He whispered something back that I couldn't understand.

The whole room was singing. We all kept playing. But I couldn't stop looking at the stranger in scarves.

Halfway through "Paradise," I couldn't take it anymore.

"Who is this guy? Get him out of here!"

This time I hear him perfectly: "Dude! It's Billy Ray Cyrus!"

Welcome to Hollywood.

⌄

I hate the word "supergroup." It's a cheap way out.

Lazy journalists love to put tags on things to sum up a whole genre or movement with a one- or two-word phrase that will make their job a little easier. If the tag can take a little backhanded swipe at a band—even better. We've seen this a million times: "stoner rock," "grunge," "indie," "hair metal."

The supergroup tag is something Velvet Revolver had to deal with in our first year. Fans never called us a supergroup, mind you, only the journalists. To label an act a supergroup suggests that they were formed for the sake of cashing in on their superstar power.

Critics couldn't handle the fact that a few of us from an internationally famous band (GN'R) were getting together with the lead singer of another internationally famous band (Stone Temple Pilots) to make music together because we love the results. To them, GN'R + STP = $$$.

But let's be frank: when you have been playing music in successful bands for a while, your friends and comrades in the field are others like you. These are the people you know! Enough with the tags! Enough with the hate! You're better than that!

Kings of Chaos is a supergroup.

It's a chance for a bunch of us old-school musicians to get together with our friends and jam. It's a conglomeration of rockers who had hits in the '70s, '80s, '90s, and '00s who go out and play huge shows in faraway places. And we get paid.

There is me, Slash, Matt Sorum, and Gilby Clarke from GN'R, Joe Elliott (Def Leppard), Glenn Hughes (Deep Purple), Corey Taylor (Slipknot), Ed Roland (Collective Soul), Dave Kushner (Velvet Revolver), Steve Stevens (Billy Idol), and Myles Kennedy (Alter Bridge). We play songs from all of our collective catalogs—from "Smoke on the Water" to "November Rain." It's a blast.

We're all professional business travelers—to say the least—and know how to pack and prepare for international business (I've already told you about my tender skin). So we were at the Avalon warming up for a tour of South America. There have been times in my life when a tour of South America with some of these guys would be enough to send me into a panic attack and a bottle of vodka. That night, I couldn't have been more excited.

⌣

I went through my twenties with a scorched-earth policy. Most of us don't have the tools or experience to deal with personal carnage that a busy and ever-changing life of being young can bring. I could have just written people off, and they very well could have done that back to me. Especially my good friend Gilby.

In the maelstrom that ensued after GN'R's *Use Your Illusion* tour, Gilby was somehow chucked from the lineup. I say "somehow" because, in all honesty, I don't remember precise details about the second half of 1993 and the beginning of 1994. All I know for sure is that we had a new Guns N' Roses pinball machine.

I don't intend to get into a whole video game versus pinball machine war here, but it's hard to deny the romance of the blinking lights of a pinball machine. The sound of the pinballs dropping into the catch still raises the heart rates of us '70s kids. We can still picture the other kids gathering around the glass as we took our turns. If you were good, you gave off a Steve McQueen–like mystique. The kids who were good at pinball got laid more (kind of like video gamers of today, right? Oh, wait . . .).

Slash was always one of those Steve McQueen–like pinball studs. He was good at every pinball game out there. Not that this should come as a surprise: whether it's guitars, snakes, dinosaurs, or pinball, Slash studies and excels at the things he is passionate about.

Sometime during the *Use Your Illusion* tour, Slash—a collector as well as a player—hooked up with manufacturer Data East, and the idea of a Guns N' Roses game started getting floated around.

We grew up with some great pinball machines. The *Playboy* machine was epic. The Rolling Stones had one. KISS had one.

There were gambling-themed games and Western-themed games. For our band to actually be entered into a conversation of having our own game was a *totally* cool and unbelievable step in our otherwise totally unbelievable ride up the rock-and-roll escalator.

Like I said, I wasn't very conscious at the time, but I remember going to a recording studio in the San Fernando Valley to do voice-over sound bites for the game (the "oh, dude!" when you lose a ball is me . . . I think). McBob laid down an introduction for the game the same way he ushered us onstage every night: "Of all the bands in the world, this is definitely one of them!" McBob has a huge, deep voice and can sound exactly like the guy on one of those monster truck radio commercials. McBob also has a very dry sense of humor and would change up his intros of the band to fit certain opportunities. For example, when we were late to take the stage, McBob would announce us as "the band that put the *punk* in punctuality."

Slash worked hard on the design of the game and was rightfully proud of the finished product. I was blown away when the machine showed up at my house (we each got one for free). I still have it, and it has a little plaque in the bottom right-hand corner with my name on it.

The game was designed after Izzy Stradlin left the band and Gilby started playing with us. It's obvious that it was a forgone conclusion that Gilby would be in the band for keeps, as his picture was included on the big mural of the band on the game. Ah, but rock bands can be a fickle bitch, and Gilby, in a flash of confusion and a hiccup of GN'R growing pains, suddenly wasn't in the band anymore.

Gilby, pissed off for sure, sued us for using his likeness on the machine. I remember thinking back then that this was a point when Gilby rightfully could have written me off (for life) for not standing up for him, and I could have just carried on without him in my life ever again as well. I think we both did that for a while.

There was a lot going on. My drinking began to drive Matt Sorum and Slash away from me. After the *Use Your Illusion* tour, even though Gilby was out of GN'R, he kept on playing live with Matt and Slash for a project they had all just finished (Slash's Snakepit). I guess I could have resented that, and they could have just kept resenting me.

In the US, we are all told that at eighteen years of age, you are an adult. For me, real adulthood didn't come until I was thirty-one. I had no idea how to take responsibility for my actions before then. I'm still trying to figure it out.

It came to me all at once, up onstage at the Avalon: "I like these guys!" I thought. No, I love these guys. I've passed some of life's most momentous mile markers with Slash, and Gilby is a good guy and great friend. Matt and I sometimes fight like cats and dogs, but at the bottom of it all, we have sincere respect for each other. We can all be motherfuckers from time to time, but that's life. When I became an adult, I made a concerted effort to repair my friendships with these guys.

Resentment is a brutal thing. In the first year or two after I got sober, I found myself swimming in a dense, black swamp of resentment and regret. I heard stories about my-self in which I was the punch line. I started to recognize what alcoholism had kept me from doing, from experienc-ing. My peculiar life path at the time, though, led me to a martial arts discipline that dealt with taking responsibility for your own actions and bettering yourself for yourself.

Self-discipline and self-respect were completely new ideas to me. I was desperate for a new way of living, and because I was (and still am) is such awe of how much at peace my martial arts teacher was, I followed his instruc-tion to the extreme. I wanted just a little part of that peace. Working past regret and resentment was key to me actually liking myself. The more I liked and trusted myself, the less I blamed others. I stopped thinking about what could have been and focused on the things I could do now.

But that was just my own personal story, and these three guys had found their own way past some of the resentments and regret. We all eventually became friends again, played in bands together, and found ourselves in faraway places play-ing great rock songs together, in front of a ton of people—with Billy Ray Cyrus in support.

STAY HUMBLE

"The mark of the immature man is that he wants to die nobly for a cause, while the mark of the mature man is that he wants to live humbly for one."

—J. D. SALINGER, *Catcher in the Rye*

DESPITE THE WOES FACING THE MUSIC INDUSTRY, IF your band is a large draw, there will still be a red carpet and moist towelette waiting. After a while, you get used to it.

Kings of Chaos draw a large audience, and our accommodations are top of the line. Not only do we get to stay in fine hotels and drink expensive nonalcoholic beverages, we get to lie down during our flights (not like that, guys). Flying in lie-down business-class seats is part of the art of arriving fit, rested, and ready for a gig.

I never used to think about dealing with jet lag and all of that rot. In your twenties, you can beat the shit out of your body every day and bounce back.

Don't get me wrong, I can still bounce back. But now I rely on preparedness, rest, and a fitness of body and mind. In rock bands, you can't use age as an excuse. There are too many people who will instantly give you shit for an "oh, my back" quip. Out here, nobody cares that you're about to turn fifty (Lemmy still addresses me as "ya young punk!"). It's antiaging by peer pressure.

There are no direct flights from Los Angeles to Asunción, Paraguay, so the flight that Matt, Slash, Gilby, and I were on had a layover in Panama City. The flight was at night, and I assumed the layover would be an hour or two, which would fit in nicely with my rest/fitness/lie-down seat plan for being ready for the gig. I could sleep on this flight after a great workout beforehand and be all set. Except these seats didn't lie down, and I can't sleep sitting up.

Matt sat next to me, and he was having the same problem. I saw Gilby kind of sleeping, and I got jealous. Slash? He is a true craftsman. He has turned sit-sleeping into an art form and long mastered the ability to quickly find the button you have to turn off when traveling. Back in row 4, I sat with envy.

As we flew the seven-hour trip to Panama, I tossed and turned, and finally gave up. I found some comfort in the fact that I'd be able to sleep after the layover, on the second leg of our journey. When we arrived in Panama City, I learned that our layover was not one but seven hours.

Even when you travel in fancy mode, travel is still travel, and a seven-hour layover sucks. I've learned to mentally check out when I travel. You can't fight what gets in your way. I've waited on tarmacs for upwards of five hours. I've had countless weather delays and flight cancellations. A seven-hour layover wasn't going to kill me.

So I looked on the bright side: this is the sort of tour that affords me the opportunity to fly my family out. Since we'd be touring through Thanksgiving, Susan and our girls— Grace and Mae—were going to meet us in Mexico City, where we were to enjoy a Mexican version of Thanksgiving dinner. Plus, the current travel day would end in a very nice hotel in Asunción with a killer gym. I wasn't about to complain—especially not in front of Matt, Gilby, and Slash (not that he'd be awake to hear it).

It occurred to me during our flight that this was the *Use Your Illusion* version of GN'R (with one obvious exception). As we sat in Panama City, I realized that this was the first time the four of us had traveled together to South America since our last GN'R gigs in 1993. The fans in Paraguay remain attached to the thought of GN'R and what we did back then. In fact, I think the lore has grown a bit.

When we got off the plane is Asunción, the police met us at customs. They explained that there were a thousand kids waiting out at baggage and they were very emotional. Our local security guys would guide us through a police line that was set up at the last minute. Our vans would be waiting right outside the doors, and security would get our luggage for us. They weren't sure how long they could hold the kids back, so we were instructed to go directly to the vans.

They seemed very serious. Shit. OK. Got it. Head down and go forward. Don't stop. Straight to the vans.

When we came out through the sliding smoked-glass doors of the customs area, chaos ensued. We clutched our backpacks as kids broke through the police line. None of us were expecting to get our hair and clothes pulled at. Apparently the *Use Your Illusion*–era GN'R guys have still got some pull down south.

We got to the vans and hurried to our hotel. I called Susan, but these are the things that I try not to tell her too much about. I don't want her to worry, so I just say, "OK, babe. So, I made it here alright . . . and I love you and miss you already."

I love to play music and am fortunate to have a fierceness for rock and roll deep in my cellar, festering and needing the light from time to time. I love playing in a band, and I've been really fortunate with the gentlemen that I have gotten to share a stage or a rehearsal room with. All the other stuff—the screaming fans, the complimentary Perrier—doesn't really matter when it comes to what I do this for.

I haven't always felt this way.

For six months after the first GN'R record, *Appetite For Destruction,* finally took off, I really thought that I was a little better looking and funnier than I had previously been given credit for. People were laughing at all my jokes! The opposite sex was suddenly all up in my business. I was the "it" guy. People finally understood how cool I was. It was about time!

Then, one of my older brothers came down to visit me in LA. After witnessing this buffoonery for a couple days, he sat me down and gave me the "you-know-these-people-just-want-to-hitch-themselves-to-you-and-your-band-and-could-really-give-a-damn-about-you" talk. I woke up. I had been drinking the Kool-Aid. It's easy to do. Especially for rock-and-roll bands.

One of my favorite "deep thoughts" on the topic occurred when one of my other bands, Loaded, was opening for Alice Cooper a number of years back. After one particularly successful show, we got to talking about Bon Jovi. In the song "Wanted Dead Or Alive," the claim is made that "I've seen a million faces, and I've rocked them all." All? Let's ponder.

I have no doubt that Bon Jovi had played to a million people by the time "Dead or Alive" was released on *Slippery When Wet* in 1986. But did they rock them all? Couldn't it be that some dudes brought their girlfriends to the show and weren't necessarily into their music? What about some parents? Or maybe some people just didn't get rocked? Hey, it's happened to me. I've gone to gigs properly prepared to get rocked and it just didn't happen.

I carried this conversation forward to one of Seattle's illustrious and beloved indie-rock front men, Death Cab for Cutie's Ben Gibbard. He said his band had actually had this very same Bon Jovi discussion. The Death Cab guys even wondered if they had maybe played to "a million faces." There was one thing they were sure about: they hadn't rocked them all.

But how could they even be sure? They had played a bunch of festivals, and you KNOW that not everyone was there to see their band. They had probably converted some of those people into new fans, but rocking them all would be a huge overstatement.

And what about me? I mean, in my whole career, I have certainly played to a ton of faces (I'll let you do the math), but, hell, I was hammered for a couple of those years and probably wasn't concentrating on faces at all. Besides, how can you see all of the faces that you play to, hammered or not? Lights are in your eyes! It's dark! You have shades on!

When you headline a smaller venue with, say, 850 people, you can actually see all of the faces in the room. But even if all of those people are there to see your band and have spent their hard-earned money to come and spend the evening with you, isn't it possible a few of those people were disappointed? I guess "I've seen 48,000 faces, and I rocked close to 41,000 of them" (a good damn percentage, by the way) is not so poetic.

Of course, this isn't meant to be a slight to Bon Jovi, and the same question could be asked about things I've stated in song. I mean, in the GN'R song "It's So Easy," was *everybody* really trying to please me? Or was it just the people I was personally coming across at that time?

You see what I'm getting at here? I don't care what your business is. You may have seen a million faces, but it's important to remember that you didn't rock them all.

GIVE THANKS

THE SHOW IN PARAGUAY WAS AT A RACETRACK CALLED the Jockey Club. We all got to the venue a few hours early to warm up. We wanted to be on the top of our game for each other. The talent level in this band is world-class, and no one wants to be the guy who fucks up a song. Sitting backstage, we started to hear a rainstorm. It turned torrential.

Since it's a racetrack, the grounds are primarily dirt, which quickly turned to mud. The crew covered all the gear onstage, and we braced ourselves for the certainty that no one would show up in this weather. We were totally wrong. Tropical storms don't phase South American rock fans, and when we opened the set with Deep Purple's "Highway Star," more than 18,000 fans were there to dance along.

Paraguay has a very young audience for rock and roll, and you could see teenagers' eyes getting huge as we came out.

There were banners and tears and very loud cheering between songs—all the things you want to see when you're up onstage.

The set list was stacked with hits from GN'R to Deep Purple, Billy Idol, Collective Soul (during rehearsals for the tour, I was pleasantly reacquainted with all of the great songs that Collective Soul had put out), Def Leppard, Velvet Revolver, and Stone Sour. It's really fun to put together a set of songs where you kind of look forward to playing the next song more than the last. The singers chose some other songs outside of our own groups to do, too, which is how we got to do Queen's "Tie Your Mother Down" and Zeppelin's "Communication Breakdown" and "Immigration Song."

Since we aren't a full-time band, Kings of Chaos always feels like it's in the honeymoon phase of a band relationship, so we just get to enjoy each other.

Matt Sorum is a wonderful guy and a terrific drummer, but he'll be the first one to tell you that he has the typical "drummer-who-wants-to-be-a-front-man" bug. Kings of Chaos is an invention and product of Matt's mind. He worked his ass off to get all these guys together, find promoters in different territories in the world who would buy this thing, and figure out travel and accommodations for all of us precious little artists. Kings of Chaos gives Matt the opportunity to be the master of ceremonies for the night, and his chest puffs out as he comes out in front of his drums, grabs the main microphone, and addresses huge audiences. All of us know Matt has worked hard on these things, and all of us sort of chuckle as we see Matt become the "front guy" he always wanted to be. And he is *great* at it.

Joe Elliott is a funny bastard. Great guy, don't get me wrong. He is one of those singers who never really got a huge ego. But he never starts a conversation with me without first calling me a cunt.

The word "cunt" is awful sounding to us Americans, of course. But in the UK, it's almost a term of endearment. Motörhead has a cook on the road named Ritchie. If Ritchie *doesn't* address you as "ya caaant" (you cunt), you know you haven't got in good with him yet.

Joe has a radio show based out of London, and he is one of those guys who takes pride in his knowledge of the history of rock music. His sense of humor is sharp and always on. Coupled with his intellect, Joe has the ability to constantly bust your balls. But he is also a world-class front man, and watching him own a crowd of 18,000, I never know whether to stand in awe or slap him in his nuts. Yes, these are the things we're really thinking about as we play along.

We played an encore of "Sweet Child O' Mine" followed by, funny enough, "All the Young Dudes" by Mott the Hoople. The whole crew came out to wrap things up as the crowd sang along at the end of an evening that was an enormous success.

There was a spring in my step the next morning, because I knew that I was a day closer to meeting my girls in Mexico City. Susan and I planned for their flight from LAX to land in Mexico City near the time that Kings of Chaos would be getting into town. Logistics are everything when you're on tour, and, Mexico City being big and sometimes dangerous, I wanted be there when they landed. Plus, I love the anticipation—waiting and searching for the first sight of Susan. At five foot nine with blonde hair, she has a tendency to stand out, especially in a place like Mexico.

I've always had a romantic idea of family life. Even during my times of trial and extreme drug and alcohol use, I held out hope that one day I'd be that guy who was the head of a family—the steady guider, the calm and strong voice. As a consequence, I am a hopeless romantic when it comes to my wife and two daughters. The imagery that has been forever ingrained in my head by It's a Wonderful Life will never leave. My girls think I am totally corny, but I don't care. I am who I am. I can get bummed out sometimes when things don't work out like they did for George Bailey, but waiting for my family at the airport filled me with joy.

We'd all been looking forward to experiencing Thanksgiving dinner in a foreign land, and now everyone from Kings of Chaos would be joining us. I grabbed my ladies and whisked them off to the hotel.

Mexico City is absolutely huge, and the St. Regis Hotel was an hour and a half from the airport. But we were in no rush, just happy to be together.

Sitting in the car, I thought about the fact that after the family's three-day stay with me in Mexico, I'd have to peel off to Europe for a nineteen-day tour with the Walking Papers, a new(ish) band of mine. The tour weighed heavily on my mind as we rolled through Mexico City in our promoter-provided black Cadillac SUV on Thanksgiving Day. I was thankful to be with them, but I was already dreading having to be away. I wanted to make every minute of this visit count.

We talked and laughed and joked and saw some incredible city sights on the way in. Our hotel was totally fancy and incredible, and our adjoining suites were world class. Listen: we'd be happy pretty much anywhere as long as we were together, but all this extra-fancy stuff was fuckin' sweet.

The beds were impossibly comfortable, and the hotel manager left us fresh fruit and a handwritten note—quite a nice touch. Even a jaded traveler like me appreciates the little things, like the button on the phone to ring "Butler Service," even if I couldn't bring myself to try it. The view included what had to be every inch of Mexico City, and I couldn't help but think that it really couldn't get more pimpin' than this.

My ladies are excellent travelers, and you'll never catch them pulling rookie moves like leaving a belt on through the x-ray machine or forgetting a passport. But I don't think they realize that if they leave clothes at home, they'll still be there when they get back. Each of their suitcases for a three-day stay dwarfed my monthlong bag by half.

But I don't complain. This is part of the fun for them—the bags, choosing what to wear. I mean, *which shoes will go with the purse that I think I should bring tonight? If I wear those shoes, should my hair be up or down? If you show skin in one area, don't show it anywhere else. Do I look hot in this? Is this outfit "indie"? Is this outfit Tumblr-ready? Totally have to take photo! SO cute! "Mom! Don't put that on Instagram!!!"*

I sat, listened, and smiled. My black T-shirt, pants, and boots were on for a good ninety minutes before the girls were ready. I've learned to be proactive with this extra time. I applied some man-perfume when it started to lose its potency. I scanned some baseball scores, put a new bed together, and painted the exterior of the house. . . . Well, I could have. If I ever speak at one of those writing workshops where people ask when I write, I'll simply point to times like these.

We met the rest of this band for dinner in an überfancy restaurant at the St. Regis. The fine-china plates were five deep (I always thought this a waste of clean dishes, but, hell, I grew up in a house of ten and without my baby fingers wrapped around a silver spoon). I do like the elegant stuff and have gotten to know how to handle myself with the classiest. And now I'd be really classy in the company of family and friends.

It's common knowledge that teenagers have a hard time adjusting to adult company. They think we are all so damn boring. It's an awkward time for kids this age, and I remember it well. I tell my kids, "Just try to not be too bored," but even I know it's a futile suggestion. As parents, all we can do is wait for the teen years to pass.

Our girls picked the best time ever to start coming out of the awkward stage.

Matt talked to Grace and Mae about an animal foundation he volunteers for, and they fully engaged back—even before Susan and I could brace ourselves for their public eye rolling at "those boring adults." Glenn told stories about hanging with David Bowie in the mid-'70s. Grace was just getting really into Ziggy Stardust and was struck by the relevance of Mr. Glenn Hughes. "You know David Bowie?!" she blurted out, completely enthralled.

Most of the guys have kids of their own and were delighted to have Grace and Mae at the dinner table. My girls do have great manners, and suddenly all of these old dudes seemed really, really cool to them (Note: I didn't say that Susan or I was cool).

"Thanksgiving dinner" was a highfalutin, five-course affair. Family-style turkey dinner was replaced by posh, small-portion sweet potato puree à l'orange and smoked duck. Like the end of A Christmas Story, we all laughed and had fun in this foreign interpretation of a traditional day. By the time we all went upstairs to go to bed, the girls were actually pretty psyched to see their new friends perform the next night (naturally, the fact that I was also playing was of little interest).

We played the Palacio de los Deportes to 15,000 people. In the middle of the gig, we broke down for a mini acoustic set that featured Steve Stevens playing a mind-numbing flamenco guitar. My girls were off side stage rocking hard when Matt suddenly invited Grace up to sing backup on our take of Bob Dylan's "Knockin' on Heaven's Door." He introduced her as my daughter, and the crowd went crazy. Grace was so taken aback that she cried in happiness for a few minutes afterward. It was a very good night.

Grace had just started writing songs and had performed live twice in front of small audiences. Singing onstage that night inspired her to get serious about starting a band, the Pink Slips. The bug has bitten her. I was thrilled to see her find something she loved. That it's something I can also speak knowledgably about—and could possibly bring the two of us closer—felt incredible. I couldn't have been prouder.

⌣

Before our family day got started the next morning, we had to circumnavigate a few hundred fans in front of the hotel. They are very passionate in these parts, and I've learned that if you just try to talk to them a bit, they'll be cool and won't follow you around. I was with my family after all, and family is something they really understand and respect in Mexico.

We had an armed security guard with us, and I told the fans outside, through an interpreter, that I'd happily sign stuff when I came back from our day out. "But I can't do photos. OK?"

The no-photo thing may seem like an asshole move. If there had only been a few people, I'd have no problem doing photos. But hundreds of pictures would have taken hours: iPhones are turned off, people want reshoots, batteries die, and lens caps are left on. I've been through this before, and I wasn't going to chew up valuable time with my family because someone's eyes were closed in a photo. Sorry.

Susan always has very specific plans written out when we travel. She is the absolute queen of researching cool stuff for us to do. That girl will record Rick Steves's travel shows and research the best sights, museums, castles, and churches for us to see in every town. When momma has "the list," we all know it's gonna be a busy day. (One time in London, we saw the David Bowie exhibit, Churchill's War Rooms, AND took a train and toured Windsor Castle, all in one day!)

We set out by foot, and our first stop was a street taco stand she had seen on Anthony Bourdain that's popular with Mexico City's business set. We saw swarms of men and women in their business attire gathered around open carts of cooking meat. We got in line with our armed guy, and no one really looked twice at us. I think armed guards are somewhat commonplace in the city.

We ordered up different tacos and sat there in the street gorging ourselves on the local fare. It was all delicious, and it felt good to be eating with the locals.

We continued our walk through a huge park with a statue that meant something about someone to some other people. We looked and nodded as our armed guy tried to explain to us the importance of the place. He forgot that we didn't speak Spanish, but we could tell that his tone was serious and full of deference, so we nodded along respectfully.

Onward, we plowed through a street of artisans hawking handmade trinkets, dolls, and bootlegged goods. We bought some stuff to take home as gifts and kept walking.

When we got back to the hotel, there were still a couple hundred fans waiting, and I asked them to line up so that I could sign stuff in a somewhat orderly fashion. "Just one photo?" I heard from my right. I tried to explain through the interpreter that if I took one photo with this particular guy, it wouldn't be fair to everyone else. The photo-asker nodded in understanding, and then said, "Yes, but one photo please?" This happens a lot.

I'm always appreciative that people are supportive of something that I am part of. I get it. I am a music fan and always have been. I snuck backstage to see the Clash in 1979. I went to the Girlschool in-store signing at Tower Records in Seattle in 1981. If I'd known where Aerosmith was staying on the *Rocks* tour in 1976, I'm sure I would have tried to hang out there and get an autograph. So, indeed, I get it, and I'm always appreciative and try to act nondickish. So I signed some of the really cool gear while my girls waited for me.

The irony is not lost on me: there are literally hundreds of people who want a picture with me, all standing right there, and Susan and I can't get our own daughters to do one goofy tourist shot with us.

We spent the evening together at the hotel, ordering in room service and just simply having awesome family time.

In the morning, I had to leave quite a bit earlier than they did. I always hate this time. I try to be upbeat and nonchalant about leaving them, but it hurts. I'm fine on my own, and I can get a lot of shit done, but for idyllic guys like me who love their wife and kids so much that it hurts—leaving sucks.

In the morning, I kissed my daughters, and hugged and kissed my wife. I told them all that I loved them more than life. They all walked me down the hall. I pressed Lobby in the elevator, and they were gone.

DON'T BE AFRAID TO GET YOUR HANDS DIRTY

L AST WEEK I WAS GRUMBLING BECAUSE MY BUSINESS-class seat didn't recline all the way. Yesterday I was staying at the St. Regis Hotel in Mexico City with my family, playing for tens of thousands of fans who knew the words to every song we played.

Today, I'm in Dusseldorf, Germany. There are no fans clamoring for a picture. No armored guards. No promoter ready to send a chauffeured Cadillac. There isn't even a hotel room. I'm sitting in the hotel lobby for the van that will be my home for the next three weeks. I'm sick as a dog.

I was bitten by the music bug before I can even remember. Most of my earliest memories involve music. And I can still vividly visualize two dreams I had before the age of ten that had a profound impact on me.

In the first dream, I'm an Iggy Pop–like singer, rolling around the stage in broken glass, oblivious to the pain. I'm all encompassed by the sound of loud guitars and booming drums around me. This performance is in the basement of our church, which would have been the only place I would have seen anything close to live music at that point. I know. Weird.

In the other, I'm in a folk band with all of my brothers and sisters—all eight of us—and we are so badass. In reality, I didn't even know how to play a G chord, but in this dream I am playing guitar effortlessly. Our family band is huge. I woke up thinking it was all so real. I was so young that it took me half a day to realize that the dream was just a dream.

A lot of my peers who have spent their lives playing music were struck by the same beautiful and damning malaise that never went away. It's a lifelong malady that will keep some of us churning and writing songs until the day we die.

I never meant for Guns N' Roses to break up. We were just getting started. But that setback—stepping away from one of the biggest bands in the world—did not stop me from playing music. It was never the fame thing that made me want to play music. It was those dreams I had as a boy. Music had me. I'm a lifer. So I started over. And when you're starting a band—like any other business—you start from zero and build from there. You start in the van.

⌣

My brain was adjusting to the move from the high-energy Kings of Chaos set of music back to the groove of the Walking Papers, so I listened to our record a couple of times while I adjusted to the fact that I'd be wifeless and kidless for the next couple of weeks.

I thought about getting in the hotel gym right then and there to try to shock and sweat this sudden onset of fever and chills out of my bones. But the German gal behind the reception desk barked that the "Gymnasio eez CLOSED!" OK, OK. Take it easy, overaggressive lady. I don't think she liked the fact that I was just hanging out in the lobby without a room. There was no place to go and absolutely nothing to do. No TV. No newspapers in English. No city nearby. My fever was getting worse by the minute.

One of the most frequent questions I've been asked since I left GN'R in 1997 has been, "How does a guy go from Guns N' Roses to [insert regular life experience here]?"

When I went to college after GN'R, I was asked a million times, "How does a guy go from Guns N' Roses to a college classroom?" People assumed a lot of things about that band, and yes, we were a big band. But what being in a big band meant to me was that a lot of people liked our music. Period. I was honored that so many fans came to our gigs and bought our records. I loved those songs we wrote, too. But we were just regular guys. And we knew it. My dream of going to college was finally realized in the late '90s, and I was as stoked about going to Seattle University as I had been about any other high point in my life.

I've also been asked, "How does a guy go from Guns N' Roses to changing a diaper?" It ain't gonna change itself. "Why is a guy from Guns N' Roses getting into the ring as a sparring partner for Sugarfoot Cunningham?" He can't be champion without help from his gym mates. "The guy from Guns N' Roses has a column for ESPN?" I like sports, too. And, well, I went to college! "Why is the guy from Guns N' Roses in the emergency room with a broken nose?" Surely you've seen the way Pete "Sugarfoot" Cunningham can throw a punch.

So, how can the guy from Guns N' Roses go from the St. Regis Hotel, playing before tens of thousands of fans, to a van in Germany?

This isn't my first time trying to break a new band. Some people assume GN'R arrived as a huge rock-and-roll entity. Of course we didn't. We had to do it just like every other band: broke, starving, and playing small clubs to no one.

Even after GN'R went multiplatinum and started selling out stadiums, I couldn't just start a new band and expect the same level of success—GN'R was a once-in-a-generation thing.

So, to get back to your question: if you have to ask why I would spend a month in a van touring Europe with a fever, then you've obviously never heard the sound of Jeff Angell's voice.

⌣

I was just finishing a tour campaign for the last Loaded record when I got a call from Jeff, asking if I would play bass on a couple songs he'd written with drummer Barrett Martin. I jammed with Barrett a lot back in 1997 and slated him as a guy I wanted to make music with in the future. And dig this: Jeff Angell was the very first guy I thought of back in 2003 as Velvet Revolver started to look for singers before Scott Weiland came into the mix. Jeff is, hands down, one of the best songwriters, lyricists, and singers out there.

Would I play bass on a few songs you guys want to record? Hell yes.

Barrett has his own independent record label, Sunyata, that he uses to release jazz and world music recordings. Jeff and Barrett were going to put this record out on Sunyata and enjoy the process of making good music without the complication and stress of trying to find a major label deal and actually forming a full-tilt band. None of this mattered to me, of course. I was just happy to be playing with two guys I'd admired for years.

There are some posh recording studios left in this world, the kind of places the public envisions recording studios should look like: high ceilings, plush rugs, and a full staff of engineers and assistants at the ready to fetch dinner for the artists. But recorded music doesn't generate the kind of money that it used to. So artists and bands are ever on the lookout for places they can record for next to nothing. A basement with a few microphones and a Pro Tools setup is increasingly the norm.

When I went to play on those first Walking Papers songs, I noticed that the studio shared a paper-thin wall with a rock-and-roll karaoke bar. The wall was so thin, in fact, that I couldn't immediately discern what I was trying to hear through the speakers in the studio and what was going on next door. Jeff was on coffee and buzzing around me, excited with a million ideas. Barrett was calmly trying to tell me where the verse and the chorus of the songs met. I couldn't really hear any of it over the chorus of "Crimson and Clover" coming from next door. I asked what key the song was in and did my best.

I thought the day was going to be a wash and that I would have to come back another time when the locals weren't shouting "Hollaback Girl" next door. So I was surprised when Jeff sent me a mix of those songs. "You actually used what I played?" Barrett has such a clear drumming groove and Jeff's guitar riffs are so deliberate and angular that through all of the noise and caffeine-fueled chaos, the chemistry of the three of us forced its way to the top. We added Ben Anderson on keys that week and watched the thing bloom.

Word of the recordings got out in Seattle, and we were offered a set at the Capitol Hill Block Party, a large and rather prestigious modern-music festival in town. We played the show on the floor of some retail space that was completely packed. Jeff and Barrett are absolute heroes locally, and luckily a few of my friends came to check us out, too. When Barrett put the record out a few weeks later, gig offers from up and down the West Coast and a tour of the UK started coming our way. It all felt so natural and cool that we said yes. We wrote new music at sound checks and became a better band every minute we played together.

After we accepted a choice spot on the touring Uproar Festival, we were approached by the Loud and Proud record label, who wanted to release our record again with a bigger commercial push and broader distribution.

Record deals these days are a different animal than the ones offered back in the mid-'80s or even mid-2000s. Simply put, there just isn't a lot of money going around in this area.

But Loud and Proud came through for us. They offered money to help us absorb the cost of touring; they ponied up for the cost of making the record; they even agreed to pay for a bunch of marketing and promo. They got us a publicist and a radio person, and all in all just did a pretty superb job at trying to get our record out. All they asked was that we tour our asses off. No problem: it's what we do.

⌣

The band and crew finally showed up at 2 p.m., and I tried very hard not to be pissed off at them for being late. Being mad at your tour manager, band, and crew is not a great way to start a run.

A splitter van is simply that: a van split in half. The back compartment is enclosed and houses all of the gear, and the front section has two rows of seats in the middle (usually with a table), and then the front two seats for the driver and another passenger. Cozy.

As I got into the van and sat down, I noticed that the seat back was too straight up and down. As our tour manager, Jay, drove, I reached for the seat-back lever to recline a bit, but there was no lever. A hot wave of frustration washed over my rising fever as I realized that I was going to spend the next two weeks straight upward, unable to sleep.

There weren't going to be any mints left on pillows or handwritten notes from hotel managers on this trip, but I had my bandmates and two crew guys, Paul and Rob. They're a great bunch of fellas, and not a diva or dick in the bunch. Though I had a rough start to the day, I was looking forward to opening a string of dates for Biffy Clyro. It was a big step toward gaining fans in Europe, and all of us were willing to suffer a bit in the short run to try to gain a larger long-game advantage for the Walking Papers in that part of the world.

I'd played Dusseldorf's Mitsubishi Electric Halle before. To get through to the backstage/loading area, you have to drive through a phalanx of security gates, as the arena itself is attached to some sort of police training facility. There are three floors of dressing rooms, and ours shared the main floor with catering.

Opening for a bigger band means we get the openers' dressing room, and privacy kind of goes out the window when you're smack-dab in the din of everyone getting fed. Crew guys from the other two bands stopped by, as did the other drivers, the riggers, and the promoters and catering staff. It's actually quite nice, as they all wished us well. But it gets complicated when I have to change my pants (I don't wear panties).

We met Biffy's production manager, and he seemed like a really nice Scottish fella. Not to generalize, but as an overall rule, the smiling glint in a Scotsman's eye always seems to indicate that a joke or a laugh is imminent. We were told that they were ready for our sound check. There was also some talk about us going on at 8:30 and that we'd get a forty-five-minute set. Cool, cool. We are seasoned guys; we're prompt and never overplay our time limit.

We did the sound check, and our gear appeared to have weathered the trip swimmingly. The stage sounded great. We hung out and watched the opening band, Arcane Roots, fire into their set. They were really, really good, and for some reason we instantly felt a kinship with them. We all talked a bit after they murdered the stage, and we got ready to do the same.

Our tour manager, Jay Smith, a twenty-eight-year-old Welshman, took up this line of work after he crashed his motorcycle and broke his back in a Grand Prix race in Ireland. While his body healed, he still needed to work, which made these gigs perfect for him. He could drive for fifteen hours straight, move gear if needed, sell merch, settle the money on a gig, and book hotel rooms effortlessly. His forte is timeliness, and he stresses if we aren't side stage ten whole minutes before we play. We know this about him, so we started to mill around back there at about 8:20.

As the clock hit 8:30, Jay flashed his flashlight to our front-of-house sound guy, Rob Jones, to signal that we were ready. Our intro music started, and the house lights went down. We took the stage, and the place was absolutely packed. Biffy Clyro has a very ardent and fanatical fan base (think Pearl Jam) that was aware that Biffy handpicked us and gave us a rousing applause and show of enthusiasm. I suddenly didn't feel sick at all, and the gig went really well for us. It felt so good to be playing with these guys again.

We came offstage feeling pretty damn good. The stress of the day dissipated, and my energy-drink high masked my fever as we got comfortable in our dressing room.

Just then, Biffy's Scottish production manager came in all excited. Wow! I guess he really liked our band? "If you guys try to pull these shenanigan's again, you'll be off the tour!" Shenanigans? Right! Like, rocking the fuck out shenanigans. But something was off. My radar for judging things was askew because of sleep deprivation. He was pissed, but I thought he was joking, because of the whole smiling Scottish eyes thing. But no, he wasn't joking. He was absolutely irate that we went onstage without his okay. What?

Again, we are pros and went on exactly at the time he wanted and came off exactly forty-five minutes later. Apparently, he forgot to mention that *he* has to signal for house lights to go down, not Jay. I was completely insulted by this little fucker, who continued his rant. I'd never seen anything like it in all my years of touring. It took everything in me to not kick this asshole in the teeth (now, that would have been some real shenanigans). I'd traveled this far and left my family to travel home on their own. I was sick as a dog and just trying to get my band to a higher level, and this dude pulls a cheap power move?

It was pathetic. I took a breath and remembered a few things my sensei had passed on to me. Don't let this kind of energy get into your head. It's his stress coming out sideways at us for whatever reason. Forget it and move on. In truth, if there really was an issue, a professional would have gone to our tour manager first—never the band. It's just not the way things are done. I unclenched my fist and thanked the maker that I was not like this dude. But he came close to getting a beat down. And I don't get close very often.

Jay said he'd deal with it, and I knew the Biffy guys knew nothing of this guy's antics. Done.

We went out and watched Biffy Clyro after the unpleasantness and soaked it all in. Technically amazing. Great songs. The band's a ball of energy and put on a fantastic light show. They will be around for a long, long time if all is right in the world. (Check out the song "Black Chandeliers.") They are also, perhaps, the nicest dudes in rock.

The gear was loaded into the van, and that was it—we were off across Germany to our next city, some 375 miles away. Our plan was to pick up a hotel in the middle and catch some sleep. I knew I wouldn't be able to sleep sitting up, so for the next 175 miles, I got caught up with my good friends Barrett, Jeff, Ben, Jay, Paul, and Rob.

After a few hours on the road, Jay's GPS started telling us that we were near our hotel. The robotic voice barked something about exiting the freeway, but I was sure it was wrong. We were in the middle of nowhere—I'm talking forest and fields, nothing else. Except for one light on the horizon, somewhat blocked by ponderosa pines and scrub brush. Our hotel? Yes. Certainly not anything close to the Mexico City St. Regis, but when I'm not traveling with my girls, all I need is a bed.

There were no lights on in the lobby when we pulled up in the gravel parking lot. Actually, there was no real lobby, just a bunch of German words next to a phone number. We called it, and a gruff woman barked back at us in German and hung up. Yeah, definitely not top-shelf accommodations and service, but at thirty euro a night, what could we expect?

A side door opened, and we were greeted by a hostess in curlers and a weird housecoat that I thought went out of production before Reagan took office. She gave us our keys, pointed up a set of stairs, and we were in. It was 4 a.m.

I was exhausted beyond what I thought I was capable. My sickness was coming back in a brutal way. The fever was well above a hundred degrees, my bones ached, and my stomach was heaving. I got to the room that I was sharing and shoved my bag in the tiny space that separated our beds in the min- iscule room. There was a kettle with granulated coffee for the morning. OK. Caffeine will be good in three hours when we have to get up. No gym. No room service. Just us, on our own, and with our mission to kick ass on this tour. I took some nighttime cold medicine and four Advil, read one page of *The Rise and Fall of the Third Reich,* and I was out.

That was one fucking long day. Mexico City to New Jersey to Dusseldorf for a gig, then another two hundred miles to this country motel.

We all believe in this thing, and we sacrifice, because that is what it takes. Just like anything worth something in this life, you forge on through the sleet and skirmish through the bullshit.

None of us are out here to get famous. None of us expect to get rich. But it would be nice if we could get this band to a place where Jeff Angell wouldn't have to pick up a hammer every time we came off tour to pay his rent.

KNOW YOUR TUNES

(Or, the One Hundred Albums Every Man Should Own)

IT OCCURS TO ME THAT MANY OF YOU READING THIS IN the United States are likely unfamiliar with Biffy Clyro, the monstrous band Walking Papers has been opening up for in arenas across Europe. Even in our hyperconnected age, bands break in certain parts of the world years before they make a splash in others. But that's a different story.

Thinking about those of you who have never heard Biffy got me thinking: What other music that is critical to my being are you unfamiliar with? To get us all on the same page, I've compiled a list of the one hundred albums that every man must be acquainted with. I wish that you were reading this online so that we could argue about the list and you could turn me on to some of your favorite bands that I've missed. So, feel free to ping me @DuffMcKagan on Twitter, and we'll have a go at it. For now, get your headphones out.

ABBA, *Gold*: Anyone who is or has been a songwriter will surely testify to the song craftsmanship that makes up the basis of ABBA's golden, blissful sounds of the '70s.

AC/DC, *Dirty Deeds*: Along with the Saints and Radio Birdman, AC/DC kicked our asses from all the way Down Under!

Adam and the Ants, *Kings of the Wild Frontier*: The Ants' music was a great left turn for us punk kids back in the '80s. This record still holds up for its boldness in direction and songwriting.

Aerosmith, *Aerosmith*: I remember looking through an *Encyclopedia Britannica* back in '73 or so and reading that Aerosmith was America's answer to the Rolling Stones. Maybe this was an overly simplistic explanation of who they were at the time, but it certainly got me into what became a fascination with early Aerosmith. With scrappy songs like "Make It" showing the earthiness of this band, the majestic "Dream On" seems just so much bigger and more genius. Here's a kick-ass rock record from tip to stern. If you can find it, also consult *Look*

Homeward Angel—hands down the best real bootleg that I have ever owned.

Alice in Chains, *Dirt*: When four dudes from Seattle discovered a new thing of their own, they wrote classic rock songs right out of the starting gate. This first record completely annihilated everything else that was around then. *Dirt* has stood the test of time very well, too. Layne = cool. Jerry = genius. Sean = brilliant. Mike = badass. A timeless record.

The Avengers, *The American in Me*: 1977 SF punk. Hear it.

Bad Company, *Bad Company* / Free, *Best Of*: Here's something I learned just the other day: Paul Rodgers sang his first Free song at the age of sixteen. Sixteen! We've all got some catching up to do. Both of these bands should be a staple of every music collection.

Badfinger, *Badfinger*: This was a magical band with a tragic ending. Some say that Badfinger was cursed, others say that the Beatles wrote their songs for them. Whatever, they were really great.

Bauhaus, *Singles 1979–83*, vol. 1: What? No, I'm not even going to try. Bauhaus!

The Beach Boys, *Pet Sounds*: This record is the sound of a band of extremely talented people trying to find a new direction. With success! Pandemonium, both personal and public, surrounded these guys during this time of their career. Instead of saying, "Fuck it," they melted into the studio and got straight-up genius.

The Beastie Boys, *Paul's Boutique*: This record was a complete game changer when hip-hop's game needed a change.

The Beatles, *White Album*: It is an impossible task to pick just one Beatles record, of course. But this record was one of the first rock records I ever heard. It taught me to play guitar and bass, so there you go.

Jeff Beck, *Blow By Blow*: No one will ever be able to play guitar like this again.

Chuck Berry, *The Complete Anthology*: I got to see Chuck Berry for the first time when I was a sixteen-year-old punk in Seattle. The lines on his face were more punk than anything I'd ever seen.

Biffy Clyro, *Opposites*: Biffy is a Scottish band that sells out arenas in Europe for a good reason. The song "Black Chandelier" was *the* standout rock song of 2013 for me. Biffy Clyro is building steam now in the US because, hell, they are fucking fantastic. Thanks for the road trip, guys.

Black Flag, *Damaged*: When Black Flag released this tour de force in 1982, it immediately went into heavy rotation alongside a T-Bone Burnett record called *Truth Through the Night*. Inexplicably enough, these two records really complement each other!

Black Flag, *My War*: The punk-rock bible. "You say that you're my friend but you're one of them. . . . THEM!"

Black Sabbath, *Paranoid*: When I was growing up in Seattle, there was a serious divide between the Sabbath and Zeppelin fans. If you were from outside of the city, it was Sabbath. For us urbanites, it was ALL about Zeppelin. We seemed too smarty-pants for them; they seemed too butt-rock for us. We were all young and dumb and full of cocksureness. The truth is, both of these bands are just so damn different that there is no way to compare or contrast them. Actually, you can't compare any other bands to these behemoths.

David Bowie, *Diamond Dogs*: It's easy to forget that David Bowie has constantly morphed and challenged his own pop success. He's a restless soul who's never done anything twice. For simplicity's sake, I'll pick *Dogs* as the David Bowie record here. With "Rebel, Rebel" and "Diamond Dogs" as singles, this record is as good a place to start as any.

Jeff Buckley, *Grace:* My first daughter is named after this record. Yeah, that is how important this music is to me.

T-Bone Burnett, *Truth Through the Night:* Known mostly as a producer, T-Bone put out this solo masterpiece in 1982.

Kate Bush, *Lionheart:* A beautiful respite from loud guitar and thumping bass.

Buzzcocks, *Singles Going Steady:* The best singles collection this side of Prince.

Cameo, *Word Up!* This is the record where Steven Adler and I found the groove for *Appetite For Destruction.*

Johnny Cash, *The Essential Johnny Cash:* Johnny is an American classic. A true icon, and someone everyone can agree is badass. "Jackson" alone is worth the price of this record.

Nick Cave, *Murder Ballads:* Man shit.

Cheap Trick, *At Budokan:* Maybe the best live record ever. Wait. Maybe? Perhaps because they're best known for this album—a hard act for any band to follow—their shows are always something to look forward to with loving rockticipation. The Trick has never used tape at shows, and they have never gone to in-ear monitors or other new-fangled onstage technology. They play loud rock music. And no one does it better than Cheap Trick—on record or onstage.

The Clash, *The Clash*: A band for the people by the people. The Clash took the mystery and inaccessibility out of the equation for fans like me. This is one of the best records to come out of the UK ever. This record was at first an exotic and very grown-up listen for me as a young teen. Yes, some of the messages on this record have been eclipsed by the passage of time, but it acts as a majestic time capsule in those moments. Years later, when I moved to LA, Paul Simonon's bass-playing on this record helped inform my decision to make the instrument my main axe.

The Cult, *Electric*: A record that stands the test of time. Great songs. Dry recording. No gimmicks.

Dag, *Righteous*: *Vibe* magazine hailed this band as the best R&B band of the decade. No small feat, considering they're a bunch of white boys from North Carolina.

The Dead Boys, *Young, Loud, and Snotty*: I discovered this record in the summer of '79, just as my young ears were coming of age to the trashier sounds of punk rock and roll (as opposed to the English stuff of the Clash, the Damned, the Vibrators, 999, the Undertones, XTC, the Jam, the Pistols, etc.). This was the first in a long line of great records that left me wanting to break stuff.

Death Cab for Cutie, *Something About Airplanes*: This is what happened when four dudes from Western Washington University decided to see what post-post-postpunk was all about.

The Deftones, *White Pony*: This band has been plagued by a massive copycat syndrome because what they invented was so damn innovative and kick-ass.

Dr. Dre, *The Chronic*: This groundbreaking record forever reshaped the face and thump of hip-hop.

Greg Dulli: When it comes to Dulli, I gave up on trying to choose one single record or one single band he has formed. When Mark Lanegan made *Imitations* in 2012, he played me a 4-track demo of Greg Dulli's, because Mark was planning on doing a song from it. "Deepest Shade" off of that *Imitations* record is one of Dulli's throwaways? Dulli is so talented that his refuse is better than most artists' best work.

Bob Dylan, *The Essential Bob Dylan*: If you are new to this planet, *Essential* is a good place to start to get yourself acquainted with a man named Dylan. No, young-sters, Bob Dylan didn't cover Guns N' Roses' "Knockin' on Heaven's Door."

Earth, Wind and Fire, *That's the Way of the World*: Another band that gave the '70s its soundtrack.

Faith No More, *The Real Thing*: The summer this record came out, I was stuck in Chicago writing songs for what would become *Use Your Illusion I* and *II*. What a groundbreaking record this was at the time: fresh and vibrant.

Fear, *The Record*: Maybe you just know these guys from a certain notorious performance on *Saturday Night Live*. If so, do yourself a favor and give *The Record* a spin. This is LA punk at its best.

Foo Fighters, *Foo Fighters*: On this debut, Dave Grohl was finally able to realize his full talents as a songwriter, singer, and guitar player, and the rest of us reaped the benefit. He makes everything seem so damn simple.

Generation X, *Generation X*: A rock-and-roll gem. Billy Idol, of course, got a lot of attention later on as a solo artist, but *Generation X* highlighted to us musicians just how fucking good a BAND could be!

Germs, *GI*: After the Sex Pistols, the Germs took punk music to another level, where hardcore was born. This is perhaps the most important record in rock that the fewest people have heard.

Green Day, *Dookie + American Idiot*: This band has weathered time well by way of elbow grease and reinvention. No matter what genre Green Day tries out, they know that there has to be a great song at the basis of it. Sorry, can't pick just one record.

Gutter Twins, *Saturnalia*: "The Stations" alone is worth the price of the record. It's a great Sunday morning song that's a call to arms for humankind. Sorry if I seem a tad grandiose when writing on the Gutter Twins, but Mark Lanegan and Greg Dulli challenge you to think and imagine beyond yourself.

P. J. Harvey, *To Bring You My Love*: This record took Harvey to another level after her gritty stint with Steve Albini.

Heart, *Dreamboat Annie*: These ladies have rocked as hard as anyone—and for much longer than most. I once witnessed manly-man Phil Anselmo sing along to a whole Heart set in Atlantic City: dude even teared up more than a few times. Phil is a real man, and Heart is the real deal to this very day.

Hellacopters, *Super Shitty to the Max*: This band's kick-ass dirty rock and roll from Sweden perhaps saved a brand of music from extinction.

Jimi Hendrix, *Axis: Bold as Love*: I found this in my older brother's stack of records when I was eight. It was sitting all alone without a cover. I put it on and imagined that all things were possible (and realized that I had saved this music from a death of scratches). I still have that disk, and I've found a cover for it.

Billy Idol, *Rebel Yell*: *The* punk-rock singer makes it big! Billy Idol has been an important person in my life for as long as I can remember. Musically, he's always been an inspiration. But, in my dark days, he was a source of strength. He remains a good friend and mentor to this day.

Iggy and the Stooges, *Raw Power*: How can you lose here? "Search and Destroy" and "Raw Power" are two of the most dangerous rock songs of all time. This record sets a good tone for a new rocker. It'll shake out all of that bad taste in rock music. This record should act as a barometer.

Iggy Pop, *The Idiot*: I wouldn't be the one to say this is Iggy's best record (because there are so many good ones), but this collection of songs may be the fairest representation of the man at a creative high.

Etta James, *The Essential Etta James*: I didn't get into Etta until Black Flag's Dez Cadena introduced me when I was about thirty-two. She is the soul of soul.

Jane's Addiction, *Ritual de lo Habitual*: I pick this record simply because "Three Days" is among the most mind-blowing rock epics ever recorded.

Joan Jett and the Blackhearts, *I Love Rock and Roll*: My old band, the Fastbacks, opened up for JJ and the BH in a tiny club in Seattle just weeks before the single "I Love Rock and Roll" skyrocketed to number one in America. She was cool when she was playing clubs, and she remained cool through it all.

Elton John, *Yellow Brick Road*: Such an epic collection of sounds and musicianship. Many a rock road trip has been made easier for me by listening to this record on repeat.

Joy Division, *Closer*: I loved this record at first listen as a teenager. Still do.

Killing Joke, *Killing Joke*: This is a sinister and mesmerizing study in just how good a band can be. Before there was a label attached to electronic music, Killing Joke invented a genre and mastered it in the same breath. And, yes, this is a breathless record.

KISS, *ALIVE!* She's a Capricorn and I'm a Cancer! While we're on the topic of KISS, let me tell you something you don't know about Gene Simmons. He's a kick-ass dancer. Backstage on a tour of South America with a bunch of top-flight talent a couple years ago, Sebastian Bach plugged in his iPod to a rather large boom box and cranked up some Boz Scaggs followed by Sly and the Family Stone. Gene suddenly appeared and started dancing . . . really well. He did some disco dancing, the mashed potato, the twist, the hustle, and some good ol' stripper dancing. We all stood rather agape at this spectacle. The God of Thunder has real and bona fide SOUL. Who knew!?!?!

Korn, *Korn*: This band's debut was as groundbreaking as anything since Chuck Berry sang "Maybellene." Jonathon's creepy and quirky voice on top of drop C tuning took dark to a different place.

Mark Lanegan, *The Winding Sheet*: If you have yet to get a chance to hear any of Mark's solo records, do yourself the big favor now. The ferocity that is his voice and cracked soul is sure to mesmerize. Trust me on this one. *The Winding Sheet* is a good place to start.

Led Zeppelin, *The Complete Studio Recordings*: Why mess around with just one of Led Zeppelin's records when you can get the whole deal in one go? This multi-disc musical tome includes live recordings that you'll be glad you have once you go completely Zeppelin crazy. These guys created the soundtrack to my life in the '70s, and they continue to be a major part of my musical diet. Seeing these guys at the Kingdome was definitely one of the true rock moments that I have drawn upon in my professional life. I can't possibly say enough about the rhythm section of John Paul Jones and John Bonham. Shit, man, when Bonham's drum solo started, I smoked a joint, went to the hot dog line, waited in line, got my hot dog, came back to my seat, and ATE my hot dog, and Bonham was STILL doing his drum solo! Perhaps not as eloquent a picture as I was trying to portray here, but funny nonetheless!

Marilyn Manson, *Portrait of an American Family*: I first saw these guys open for Danzig around 1995. Sure, sure, Alice Cooper did this thing in the late '60s and early '70s, but Manson and his band were straight creepy and hailed from Florida's swamplands—citing mass murderers as their influences. Dark. Essential.

Johnny Marr, *The Messenger*: Once in a while you get to talk to someone or have an experience that positively readjusts your own view of things. A conversation I had with Johnny Marr (the Smiths, the Cribs, Modest Mouse) on the occasion of the release of his solo debut, *The Messenger,* was one of those experiences for me. This is a man whose position in rock-and-roll history is secure. A man who could dine out on his considerable back catalog for the rest of his life.

But he's restless. He's not done. This is a man who put out his solo debut when he was forty-nine years old! Johnny Marr is an inspiration, a kid in the candy store of life grabbing as much as he can.

Johnny didn't want to talk about whether or not his "old band" was getting back together again, and neither did I. We've both been through that before. I wanted to know where his songs came from, where his unmistakable sound came from. I wasn't disappointed.

"My family was obsessed with records," he told me. "So as a little boy, my favorite toy was a little toy guitar. So I had a thing for the guitar much younger than all of my mates. I would think about the shape of it and all of that—it wasn't for the fame and fortune or getting girls or anything, I really just loved this little wooden guitar as a boy. I would always be upgrading that."

This is a man dashing headlong into the still-mysterious and exciting arena of writing new songs and playing with musicians who inspire him. He is as excited about plugging in a guitar now as when he was fourteen years old. When Marr talks about being as inspired to make music today as he was as a kid, there's honest excitement in his voice—not the blasé and predetermined excitement of some veteran trying to simply "pimp" a new record. Johnny Marr is an original, and a damn fine gent.

Marr lived in Portland during the Modest Mouse run. He jammed with that band because he was completely mystified about what and who influenced them. His wanderlust for musical exploration leads him just as strongly now as when he was a teen taking trains across Manchester to jam with some dudes he didn't even know.

Moving back home to Manchester in 2010 with his wife and family, Johnny got a large dose of the gravity and familiarity of returning to a place of comfort and invention. The songs for *The Messenger* were born on his trip home. Johnny Marr is the anti–guitar hero: an inventor, an explorer, and a guy who seems to fully "get it" as far as his place in the mix. He is a regular guy with an irregular past—and an uncommon ability to make great music.

Curtis Mayfield, *Superfly*: Curtis Mayfield is one of the unsung heroes of the early '70s civil rights movement. His social commentary by way of song painted a vivid picture of the black inner city. "Freddy's Dead" is the best of the best.

Metallica, *Master of Puppets*: Impossible to pick just one Metallica record, but this one rocks the hardest from front to back.

Mother Love Bone, *Mother Love Bone*: This bittersweet record got me through some tough times when I found myself on the losing end of vice.

Mötley Crüe, *Too Fast for Love*: This was a rock record that all of us punkers could identify with back in '81. On the heels of Motörhead's *Ace of Spades*, TFFL opened up more possibilities for what was next to come.

Motörhead, *Ace of Spades*: When I was a youngster and Motörhead's *Ace of Spades* came out, all of us in the Seattle punk-rock scene instantly recognized the weight of the band and Lemmy Kilmister, its bassist, singer, and songwriter. They embodied all that was good and great about rock and roll: snarling vocals and to-the-point lyrics. Drummer Phil "Filthy Animal" Taylor pounded the FUCK out of the drums; Fast Eddie Clarke complemented it all with his no-nonsense and very LOUD guitar playing. Motörhead always seemed more punk than metal because they were always in on the joke. Too many other metal bands took it all much too seriously back then.

When I moved down to LA in 1984, it was the influence of guys like Lemmy, Phil Lynott, and, as I've already mentioned, Paul Simonon that steered me to choose bass, back when I was still a somewhat able drummer and guitar player. I was going to Hollywood to sort of "invent" myself, and I chose bass playing as the coolest of the rock-instrument triumvirate because, hell, it was the baddest choice back then (to me at least).

And it wasn't just my choice of playing bass that Lemmy and Motörhead influenced. Dare I say that without

Motörhead, there would have been no Metallica, GN'R, Nirvana, Alice in Chains, NIN, or everything between and after. Yeah, they mean that much. For proof, check out the documentary *Lemmy: 49% Motherfucker, 51% Son of a Bitch.*

There is a moment in the documentary where Dave Grohl states very eloquently what Motörhead means to him and the rest of us in the audience. To paraphrase, Grohl talks about the "humanness" of Lemmy. Boils and all, Lemmy lets us know that you don't have to be perfect and beautiful and polished to a shine to succeed in this life. Motörhead makes me both exceedingly happy and somehow ashamed. The happy part is obvious in that Motörhead helps us all to exorcise some demons through the art form of balls-out rock and roll. But also, watching the movie and seeing Lemmy progress throughout the film, it dawned on me that this guy has always just stuck to his guns and never bit in to a trend or a new technology, recording-wise. Most of us just sort of naturally change with the times: our style of dress, our take on life and love, the bars we go to, and all. Lemmy has changed nothing, bringing to the fore the fact that he just had it right from the beginning.

Nashville Pussy, *Let Them Eat Pussy*: This Kurt Bloch–produced masterpiece shoved a middle finger up the ass of all the band's pretenders. Greasy and bloody and fun, for sure.

The New York Dolls, *Too Much Too Soon*: This record became the bible for bands like the Pistols, the Damned, and the Clash.

Nine Inch Nails, *The Downward Spiral*: This is one of the most musically brilliant records ever made . . . ever. Trent Reznor melded technology, melody, anger, tenderness, and mystique into a continuous and digestible epic. The guy somehow finds a way to constantly get better and expand his art to this day. Incredible.

Nirvana, *Nevermind*: Since Nirvana was GN'R's label mate at Geffen, I was able to get a prerelease cassette of this record. I remember driving around LA cranking the fuck out of it. I wore out my cassette and had to get another one. I used to brag to anyone who would listen that these guys were from "my town" and that soon the rest of the world would realize that people didn't live in tepees in Seattle! Borrowing and perfecting all of the best from the punk-rock bands before them and then adding an angled angst and song craftsmanship of their own, Nirvana simply owned it all, turning on a world full of youth who could relate.

N.W.A., *Straight Outta Compton*: There are few timeless rap records from this era, but N.W.A. was more than just a band for the time. They had a message and found the sound to carry it forth. Bad as all hell.

Outkast, *The Love Below*: I played bass along to this record every night before we played on VR's first full summer tour ('04). What an amazing journey this record takes the listener on. Here is to more of this from Andre 3000!

Pearl Jam, *Ten*: A record that made personal politics and caring for others okay. Pearl Jam somehow fused kick-ass rock with a Seattle-ness and a PC ethic.

The Police, *Ghost in the Machine*: They had us at "Roxanne," but then this gigantic record came out, and the Police became a worldwide sensation.

Prince, *1999*: A by-product of the fact that I grew up in a very large family and spent much of my teen years in group environments like bands and sports is that I never had a chance to get comfortable being by myself. This caught up to me as I transitioned into adulthood.

In 1982, when I was eighteen, I went through a sea change in my life. My mom had sold my childhood home, I no longer lived with either of my parents, and I felt unrooted. I could feel the beginnings of the breakup of my first real relationship with a serious girlfriend. There were also drugs cascading into Seattle, and I was losing a lot of close friends to the pull of narcotics. I felt alone for the first time in my life.

I was a guy who played different instruments in different bands, and a friend of mine who was a big fan of Prince early on turned me on to *Controversy* and *Dirty Mind*. He thought I might relate to the genius multi-instrumentalist from Minneapolis. The records were groundbreaking and forward thinking. I was hooked.

When *1999* came out later that year, I found a respite and safe haven between the grooves of the epic double album. It didn't matter that the topics of "Little Red Corvette" and "Something in the Water" didn't directly relate to me and my situations; it was the intent and drama and impossibility of how good this record was that made me start to think that maybe ANYTHING was possible in my own life, too. I could rise and get through all this messy teenage young-adult stuff, with a little help from this record, which became the soundtrack of my life through 1983. When I decided to move to LA on my own, *1999* (by then on cassette) became my traveling companion and best friend. Since then, many records by different artists have become the soundtracks of different eras of my life, but nothing has had such an impact and given me confidence and be-alone and stay-alone capabilities. I owe a lot to this record.

Thankfully, my need and training for being alone has passed. I am a happy family man nowadays, and I find myself surrounded, all of the time, by my girls, dogs, and stinky rock bandmates. But Prince's music remains a touchstone for me, and *1999* will always hold a special place in my soul. It gave me strength, and it gave me friendship. It made me work harder for the things I wanted to attain. It was the sturdy vessel that protected me in those choppy and scary waters of my coming-of-age sea change.

Queen, *Sheer Heart Attack*: If "Stone Cold Crazy" were the whole makeup of this record, it'd still make this list. But every song of this record is the result of the forging of brilliant song craftsmanship and unmatched musical talent.

Queens of the Stone Age, *Rated R*: This record single-handedly saved rock and roll in the early 2000s. This record would have stood up against most in any era, but the timeliness of *Rated R* was a welcomed relief from the drag and hum of the crap that was going on then.

The Ramones, *Ramones*: Do I really have to say anything at all? The Ramones careened into the New York scene with nary a clue of how to play more than three or four chords. But they made those chords rip and count. "Blitzkrieg Bop" is one of the most solid rock songs ever written. The Ramones can never *ever* be overlooked for their importance in modern rock music.

Lou Reed, *Rock and Roll Animal*: This record scared the shit out of me when I was thirteen. I imagined New York as this dirty and terrifying place with heroin on every corner. But something about "Sweet Jane" inspired a hope. Imagery like this is rarely found in recent times.

The Refused, *The Shape of Punk to Come*: This is still one of the records I like to spin for the crowd before I take the stage. It's a jaw-dropping collection of angry and varied music from a group of musicians who were simply masters of their art.

The Rolling Stones, *It's Only Rock and Roll*: When I wasn't listening to *1999* during my move from Seattle to Hollywood, it was *It's Only Rock and Roll* that kept me awake on my nonstop drive and kept me company when I was lonely down there in Hell-A. This cassette and my little ghetto blaster were both stolen out of my car a couple of weeks after the move. Ah, welcome to the jungle? (Sorry, couldn't resist.) This record set the tone for what cool should sound like. "Short and Curlies"? Yeah, she's gotchu by the balls.

The Saints, *I'm Stranded*: Before the Sex Pistols made the genre popular worldwide, there was a little punk-rock band from Brisbane, Australia, writing the songs that would influence so many.

Sam and Dave, *Rhino Hi Five*: Booker T and the motherfuckin' MGs!

Screaming Trees, *Sweet Oblivion*: Another great band with Mark Lanegan on vocals, the Screaming Trees put out a bunch of fine records, so get them all. Such a different feel and intent than what was the norm back in the early '90s, and this record has withstood the test of time.

The Sex Pistols, *Never Mind the Bollocks*: This record changed the way we all thought about rock music. NEXT!!!

Slayer, *Reign in Blood*: Angel of Death!!! They don't mince words and they don't mince the rock.

Slipknot, *Volume 3*: If you have time for only one song here, make it "Prelude 3.0," a dark and beautiful epic song that showcases the power that Slipknot was just beginning to toy with.

Sly and the Family Stone, *Fresh*: This album epitomizes what groove and funk are about at their primal best. Take special note of "If You Want Me to Stay." KILLER!

Soundgarden, *Down on the Upside*: This record was the culmination and pinnacle of all of the talent that this group of men pushed and pulled out of each other during their first era. I'm so glad they're back for round two!

Spiritualized, *Ladies and Gentlemen, We Are Floating Through Space*: A great groove album to just sort of mellow yourself out with. I put the title track on when things get a little too hectic in life.

Stiff Little Fingers, *Inflammable Material*: Real unpolished OG punk with a message.

Sweet, *Desolation Boulevard*: The blueprint of rock fantasy.

The Temptations, *Greatest Hits*: Do I really need to say anything about the Temps?

Thin Lizzy, *Dedication: The Very Best of Thin Lizzy*: Oh, Rosalie! I really, really love this band. A few years ago when I was in Dublin, on tour with VR, I stumbled out of my hotel one morning in search of some coffee. As I took a sleepy turn to my left, I ran smack into a life-size bronze statue of singer Phil Lynott. When I got back to the hotel lobby, the desk manager asked me if I saw the statue of "de goy prom Tin Lizzy?" Indeed, I had.

Johnny Thunders and the Heartbreakers, *L.A.M.F.*: A whole generation of us learned to play guitar the *right* way from this record. We also learned to tuck our pants inside our boots.

The Time, *Ice Cream Castle*: Back when Prince had at least three different musical projects going at one time (Vanity 6, too), the Time was almost as big as the almighty Purple One. "Ice Cream Castles" is a lost gem and a cool summer jam. Enjoy!

U2, *Joshua Tree*: This record was not just the soundtrack to my summer of '87 but it got me through all of the craziness that was surrounding Guns N' Roses that year. My best friend died that summer, and U2 seemed to speak to me and only me, steeling my sorrow and tempering my sadness. This record still holds an important place in my heart.

Van Halen, *Van Halen*: Game changer.

The Vibrators, *Pure Mania*: With songs like "Petrol," "You Broke My Heart," and "Yeah, Yeah, Yeah," *Pure Mania* was a favorite record to put on just before we wrecked a house or played beer curling at a punk-rock house party. Punk, for sure, but also consider this one of the best pop records ever written.

Tom Waits, *Mule Variations*: What the hell is he doing in there?

Jack White, *Blunderbuss*: Creativity knows no bounds with Jack White. And while the rest of us may think that the guy just can't sit still (what, eight different band projects in the last dozen years?), success is pretty much all that he does. Jack's first true solo venture is one of those records that makes you feel like you are in the same room as the players. The sounds and riffs are authentic and hearken back to some Levon Helm/the Band-isms, sounding current and urgent at the same time. If you delve into the word choices, rhyme schemes, and subject matter of the lyrics for *Blunderbuss*, you will find a smart, dark, and hip trip into the blackness of love found, lost, and finally disposed of.

The Who, *Who's Next*: Another band that is kind of stupid to pick one record, but this one has "Baba O'Riley," soooo . . .

X, *Los Angeles*: Sometimes a record comes out that just sends everything into a new direction. Rock changed after *Los Angeles* came out.

XTC, *Drums and Wires*: The beginning of postpunk was this record.

The Yeah Yeah Yeahs, *Fever to Tell*: Great songwriting, production, and Karen fucking O!

Zeke, *Flat Tracker*: I had just left GN'R and returned to Seattle when this record came out. I felt delirious that OG punk rock had come back in the form of Zeke.

ZZ Top, *Tres Hombres*: Kick-ass American blues from down Texas way.

OK, so, that's a few more than a hundred, but, come on, you try choosing between Lou Reed and Queen!

SET GOALS (AND BOUNDARIES)

Or, How to Survive in Close Quarters on a Land-Sea Voyage

As I've gone to great pains to explain, I don't mind leaving the luxury accommodations of the St. Regis and Kings of Chaos for the splitter van and cheap hotels of the Walking Papers. I am, and always will be, a punk-rock road dog. I don't necessarily love spending 350 miles in a van, but it's something I'm used to. Through all the changes of scenery with various bands, there has been one constant: I've had my own hotel room. If I wasn't sharing a room with my wife, I wasn't sharing it at all.

That all changed on this Walking Papers tour. For the first time since 1988, I shared a room with a bandmate. The last time I had a roommate, I bunked up with Slash back when I was twenty-four years old, and neither of us really slept—we certainly weren't looking to our hotel room as a place to get, um, rest.

As GN'R became more popular and fans started showing up at our hotels, we, like many musicians, started staying under assumed names. Assumed names can be anything really, as long as it's not *your* name, so that a fan or fans can't just keep calling the hotel and asking, "Can I talk to Duff McKagan please?

Slash and I dubbed ourselves the Likesheet brothers; he was Phil and I was Luke. So, of course, we were "Phil Likesheet" (get it?) and "Luke Likesheet" (right!?!??!). The names kind of mimicked the lifestyles we were living at the time. Now, at fifty, I'm *very* far removed from that party-til-you-drop-what-kind-of-drugs-do-we-got-where's-the-girls dude. Today I'm the read-my-book-where's-the-gym-and-coffee-phone-home person.

From what I can remember, we had some fun as the Likesheet brothers. We did kid things like trashing our hotel room. We were so naïve that we thought we could totally destroy our room and then just walk away and try to claim that someone broke in and caused trouble. One time we completely decimated our mattresses and bed frames and walls and lamps and that little desk and chair. Two of our guitar techs, who were much more seasoned than Slash and I, just watched us and laughed, thinking how moronic we were for sure.

I think that trashing of the room cost us something like three grand. Even then, neither of us were holding that kind of dough, so our manager had to loan us the bread, and we slowly paid him back . . . which took months out of the weekly $125 salary we gave ourselves back then. I never trashed a hotel room again.

Having not shared a room with a bandmate in so long, I just assumed that everyone knew all of the rules of sharing a room. But no. Sometimes a band member forgets the golden rule of sharing a hotel room: poo in the lobby, not in the room.

This rule applies *any* time you are sharing a room. Wife. Girlfriend. Boyfriend. Grandma. Whatever. Be cool when you are together in a small space.

Unless your shit don't stink or you have a book of matches, pooing first thing in a shared room is one of the most offensive things to do to your roommate. Remember: he or she must now try to fall asleep with your poo-scent molecules swimming around his or her nose. Hotel lobbies always have restrooms. Use them to take care of #2. Is that so hard?

This has happened to me a few times lately, and it's hard on a traveling guy. I just sit there in my room sort of dumbfounded, before I go downstairs "to make a phone call." I'm not really making a phone call. I'm downstairs in the lobby waiting for the smell in the room to go away, as I popped the window just before I left the room.

I'm pretty sure I do myriad things that annoy others on the road. So, in this respect, I am quite sure that my shit surely does stink from time to time.

Now that I think about it, I don't remember Slash and me eating food in those early days. That probably had a lot to do with why we never butted heads on the shared-room-poo dilemma. Here are a few other pieces of traveling wisdom that I hope will be of service to all men who find themselves traveling in close quarters with one another:

Maintain personal hygiene. This is key. Crap breath and stank butt can lower morale and kill an appetite. A band needs to eat. Stinky body odor from an orifice or two can kill one's will for nourishment.

Respect off-limits places. For example, when you draw the curtains to your bunk on the bus, no one should be allowed to fuck with you. No punching in the dick, even. Each other's girlfriends/wives/husbands/boyfriends are also off-limits. Usually.

Share everything. Clothes, chocolate, drugs, whatever. If it's expendable, it is a "band" item.

Don't be serious. You will be ganged up on in no time and be the butt of every tour joke. Join in on the fun. Be the river flowing downstream, not the rock trying to hold it back.

Know some history. When you're on the road, it's always cool to know something about where you are. For instance, Dublin is in Ireland. Belfast is in Northern Ireland. Do not fuck this up (broken fingers aren't good for guitar playing). History is good tour bus conversation material, too.

Have a look around. Go out and take a walk. People and different cultures are so damned interesting. And remember: know where you are going. Getting mugged with tour-float dough ain't good for the bottom line.

Don't get stuck. If you are having a pint or five after the show, it is always a good idea to grab a card from your hotel. You don't want to go through the old "I have no idea where I am staying, Mr. Cab Driver" debacle. It's an expensive ride.

Have your shit sorted. Put all your vitamins in one bottle. Don't forget your passport, and always have a high-res photo of your band in your phone just in case there is a last-minute request from the press or a promoter. Have a kick-ass backpack for your day bag. Know where your shit is in your day bag so that you aren't the one holding up the show when everyone else is ready to leave in the hotel lobby.

Hair conditioner makes good shaving cream. So don't bring both.

Get used to being away from cozy shit and the safety of home. Bring your teddy bear if you need to. And get Skype.

Don't roam. Holy hell! Turn the data off on your phone if you are going international. Just turning on your phone when you land in, say, London can cost you like 30 British pounds (that is, like, US$10.072) when your e-mails load. Either get some cheap phone when you land at that airport or wait for Wi-Fi at the venue you are playing.

Sleep, little baby. Sleep. If one of you is sleeping, then everything is off limits. If you are that guy who wakes up a sleeper, the rule of the road is that you must get kicked squarely in the nards. No ifs, ands, or butts.

Don't poo in the same room that someone else is eating in. Unless of course said eater gives the "poo OK." If a "poo OK" is granted, you have a band that will NEVER break up, your turnover will be low, and your shareholders will earn a healthy rate of return.

If I've said it once, I've said it a thousand times: "Ass to ass, dog!" Years back, a huge security guy got ruffled when a band member passed him crotch to ass in a tight space. This security guy did not exactly dig the fact that his manhood had been compromised. He dressed down the young rocker right then and there: "Man, it's always ass to ass, dog . . . ASS TO ASS!" Whether it's a city bus or a private plane, it's always ass to ass, dog.

BE SMART WITH YOUR MONEY (AND YOUR TALENTS)

I T'S NOT THAT I CAN'T AFFORD A BUS OR A FEW PLANE tickets.

As you've no doubt noticed, my "work week" can just as easily be spent sleeping in the front of a jet as it can in the back of a van. I'm a regular resident at both the St. Regis and Motel 6.

I didn't get into this for the complimentary shampoo or the plush white robes. When I started playing music, the idea of traveling around the country in a van with a band was the most glamorous and successful experience I could imagine. If only I could be so fortunate. And I have been.

I've spent my adult life making records and traveling the world in search of an audience. This is the professional life I dreamed of before I knew this could be a profession. The van is what I aspired to. It's where I live. The jets, the hotel butler, the fancy dinners—this isn't the norm; it's an aberration and a privilege.

When we have success, it's easy—and human—to believe that the high times will last forever. It's easy to get used to the comfort. And it's tempting to give those things to ourselves, even when our circumstances do not organically provide them. This is how people go broke.

As an ardent sports fan, this is something I think about during free-agent season, when players sign contracts for hundreds of millions of dollars. We all dream that one day a whole windfall of cash just comes cascading in. Like winning the lottery. Like finding a suitcase bulging with dollars. Or getting a pro athlete–size signing bonus and contract. The day comes that we can suddenly afford anything we want. At least for a little while.

Allen Iverson reportedly made $154 million in the NBA. He was later sued by a jeweler for $375,000 worth of unpaid bills. Terrell Owens told *GQ* that nearly all of the $80 million he made in his career is gone. Even superstar agent Leigh Steinberg filed for bankruptcy.

Going broke isn't just a problem for musicians and athletes, obviously, but for anyone who doesn't take the time to look at the big picture.

Here are some factors that are not often discussed or considered:

- When you come into a box of money for the first time, words like "investment," "risk," "reward," and "money retention" are likely foreign to you. They sure were for me.

- The taxman takes half.
- Your agent takes 10–15 percent.
- Your lawyer gets 5 percent.

Suddenly $10 million looks more like $2.5 million. Still not a bad payday, eh? It's not.

But put yourself in that situation. You've got some of your boys you wanna take care of, right? Maybe put some of your buddies on a payroll? And you gotta take care of your family, and especially your mom, right? OK, so buy her a house.

And what about a car and house for yourself? You might as well get that Mercedes AMG for $200K. The house on the water on the good side of town will work . . . and you need a condo in the city that you are playing in, too.

All of a sudden, that $10 million is gone, and you are signing playing cards at a convention just to pay down that car that is now six years old, dented, and worth about thirty grand. And now maybe the real estate market has taken a nosedive.

But everyone expects you to be flush with cash, and so, to stave off embarrassment for a while, you still try to look like you are living like a king. Until you are in debt and filing for Chapter 11.

Those be the grim and cold hard unpleasantness. Those things we don't think of when we blankly daydream of a bag of signing-day cash.

I can relate. I'd love to put my bands up in the finest hotels and hire limos to shuttle them between the hotel and the gigs. They do deserve it. They do work hard for little or no money.

But, like I said, it's a good way to go broke.

REAPPLY YOUR TALENTS

Since we're talking about sports . . . when I read about the death of Junior Seau, I thought: we just lost a giant of a football player, but we also lost a guy who was good outside of football, too. He was a mentor, a philanthropist, and a good human being. At forty-three years of age, he was also just getting started.

Of course, none of us can be certain of the reasons for a person's suicide. Once in a while there is a note. Once in a while, there are clear-cut reasons that will inform us. But in Seau's case, there is just the blank emptiness of sudden loss, with no real answers.

It's a far stretch for me as a writer to try to bring anything more than assumption into this conversation. At this point, I would never want to try anything so base. Seau had a pristine reputation that he earned in his short life by being a stand-up man—both on and off the field.

But something that really must be paid attention to now is how a player is supposed to transition into "normal" civilian life after the weekly rush of the game, and perhaps even undiagnosed brain trauma.

I can speak a little bit to the former.

I had to get out of the game for a minute back in the '90s. In my case, drugs and the devil's juice were destroying me, body and soul. It was time for me to make a change, and so I sobered up and went to school.

But, as I soon found—even in the very positive environment of a college campus and having a brand-new daughter and excellent wife—you can't suddenly stop doing that thing you have such a passion for. That thing you get such a rush from (I'm talking about playing music . . . not the drugs and drink bit).

But musicians only really need to keep their musical chops up. We don't need to be in the best physical shape of our lives. Our careers can go on for a long, long time. And even if you are not playing the biggest places anymore, a musician can still get that rush and contact with an audience.

For pro athletes—and for other professions that favor youth—it's another story. When the game is done for them, it also ends a lifetime of being the top dog. From Little League to high school, and college to the pros, these guys were always the best, and they were touted as such. It has to be unthinkably tough to suddenly get cut or be put on an indefinite injured reserve list or just simply retire. There is no NFL for old guys.

And even though many pro athletes have a college degree, it is not so easy to have a second successful career, especially one with any hope of near parity in pay or lifestyle. No more free trainers and support staff. No more weekly rush of the game and urgency in life.

According to a 2006 *USA Today* article, there is more bad news:

> Experts say a high percentage of those men will be thrust into the so-called real world with few marketable skills to increase their wealth and serious self-identity issues that often make the transition from the game a perilous one.
>
> In fact, 78 percent of all NFL players are divorced, bankrupt or unemployed two years after leaving the game, according to Ken Ruettgers, a former player and current advocate for NFL players transitioning from professional sports.

We should all hope for a better way to ease our players into the afterlife of pro sports. But it's not just athletes who transition. We all do. We lose our jobs, we become unfit for the work that has defined us, or we retire. It's in times like these that we all need to consider our gifts and find ways to reapply our talents.

Even as I continued a successful and satisfying career in the music business, my years spent at Seattle University reignited my love for writing. After I was hired to write a weekly column for *Seattle Weekly*, other opportunities popped up as well: Playboy.com offered me a regular gig and later so did ESPN.com. At one point, I decided it was time to write my first book.

It's So Easy was released in 2011. And when I got into promoting the book, I realized how much of my experience promoting albums translated to the world of publishing, even if the two communities were very different.

At one point, my publisher dispatched me to something called BookExpo America in New York, a closed convention where all of the different large and small publishers show their new wares to buyers like Barnes & Noble, Borders, Amazon, Costco, Target, and Hudson (you know, the stores at the airports), as well as all of the independent bookstores like Elliott Bay, Powell's, and the like.

The night before my signing at the Expo, my senior editor and her staff threw a cocktail party in my honor at a fancy restaurant in Manhattan called Lamb (so damn posh, right?). It was actually one of the sweetest things I've ever been to.

The publishing community is VERY different from the music community. Or, to be more precise: the publishing community is like some wonderfully kitschy and nerdy indie movie. The mood and personality that filled the room at the party was interesting, thoughtful, smart, nerdy, and diverse.

I have been trained to be a little (OK, VERY!) dubious of the rock-and-roll press. They always want "the dirt" or are looking for some snidely and wise-ass way to catch me off guard or misquote me so that it seems much bolder and dumber than the things that they actually ask me about. There were members of the press at the cocktail party. I was ready.

I quickly pulled my editor aside and frantically told her that I didn't know that the press would be at this party and that I didn't want to talk to them at the risk of being mis-quoted for the umpteenth time. She looked at me quizzically and stated that "the publishing press would never dream of doing something like that!" Yeah, I guess *Kirkus Reviews* and the book side of Associated Press and whatnot don't just want the dirt. The publishing industry, it turns out, is still a quaint little field that is still in the business of actually being excited about new things, and the publishing press and all of the different publishing companies are still in the business of helping each other out. They want their industry to be strong, and there just really doesn't seem to be any sort of underhandedness and BS happening behind the scenes.

At dinner after the party, I sat with a few of the publisher's mucky-mucks, and we all talked about the books we had been reading. I had just finished *One Bullet Away* by Nate Fick, and one of the gentlemen that I was sitting with had edited that book. Yeah, that's right, for a book nerd like me, that was like sitting with the guy who had just produced the latest Rolling Stones record. Pretty cool.

At the Expo, I signed copies of my book for a thronging line of like-minded book nerds and exchanged small talk with them the same way I've done at countless album signings. There were a lot of people from other publishing companies, book buyers for large and small stores, and librarians, even one from the Seattle Public Library system, which I have frequented since I was a child.

The one big difference—and I must say that I was a tad crestfallen—was that none of them asked me to sign their tits.

It's So Easy also gave me a chance to experiment with different kinds of performances.

I did the typical book signings, sure. But I also presented sold-out evenings of music and readings at clubs and theaters around the world. I even played a stripped-down, intimate gig at the Viper Room in LA. That was an interesting night.

Before I go any further, I want to say that I think it's actually a genuinely sweet offer when someone passes me a joint. "I don't smoke weed," I say politely. I know the intent is good, so I never want to be the guy who passes judgment or otherwise looks at that situation with scornful disdain.

Drugs are a funny thing. No one really wants to get high alone, at least not when one is still in the "casual use" stage, anyway. Rarely will you hear of people doing bumps of cocaine or hits of crystal meth on their own. There'd be no one to jabber and talk mad nonsense with.

I thought that if you bought a ticket to a show in which I present the story of my pancreas exploding that you probably know that I don't do drugs anymore. Right? Apparently not.

Places like the Viper Room—and the old CBGBs, come to think of it—have only one set of bathrooms. Everyone shares. So, when I had to go, I went into the men's room at the Viper Room and patiently waited my turn. And, there I was, dick in hand, and I got offered a bump of coke.

Now listen, I will state it again: I find no fault with the people who offer me such things, it's just fuckin' odd sometimes.

If I were in my heyday of getting fucked up, these people would have offered me free drugs only once. Guys like me aren't dainty in our usage. All the drugs in that men's room would have been gone in an instant.

I guess learning to say no is a talent I picked up on the rock-and-roll circuit as well.

MAKE TIME FOR YOUR FRIENDS

Y OU CAN'T TOUR WITH YOUR BAND, IN A VAN, IF YOU don't like each other. That would be hellish. You're going to be with the same people constantly. Even when you love each other, you still need a break from time to time.

When I say break, I'm talking about taking a spell from the 24/7 tour grind that can drive anyone to the asylum. Walking Papers keyboardist Ben Anderson and I saw a chance for our escape—hey, sometimes, just splitting a band up into parts can do wonders for morale—and an opportunity to score a night off in Madrid.

Looking at a sixteen-hour drive from Lille, France, Ben and I noticed that the drive would be our one and only day off. Fuck that. Instead of spending our day off in the van, we decided to hop a European econo flight and spend the day in the beautiful city of Madrid.

It wasn't just that we needed a few hours to ourselves. Ben needed new pants, and my boots were worn through. The day off would give us a chance to take advantage of Spain's dire economy, do a little shopping, and maybe even find a good hotel gym (a welcome change from working out at cold venues, with just jump ropes and yoga mats).

Ben is a handsome man and knows how to carry himself. Being cool and confident travelers is key to a band getting along. Fitting in and going with the flow and speaking a little bit of the local tongue become second nature to world citizens such as ourselves. Ben is all of these things. He's also extremely handy. In the cab ride to the airport in France, he told me he had made us reservations at a really nice restaurant in Madrid for the following night and that the paella at this place was "to die for." A nice quiet dinner is not something you get on tour very often. I was looking forward to this getaway already.

I was pleasantly surprised by Ben's short bursts of French to the cab driver. I somehow felt safe and taken care of. I realized that Mr. Anderson had a sort of effortless debonair quality that had previously eluded me. Really nice skin, too.

Perusing the little airplane menu on the flight, Ben and I both ordered some low-fat yogurt and a bag of raw almonds. We are ultra-aware of the need to keep our girlish figures as a main focal point of our tour fitness regimes. Sure, you want to feel good and healthy out there, but, let's be honest, we want to look good, too. You know, keep them glutes high and tight (am I right, guys?), maybe a better pectoral set, and good hair and the right skin products.

After landing, Ben informed me that he had already booked us hotel rooms in the city center, right off of the stunning and picturesque Plaza Majore (Main Plaza) in the shopping and restaurant hub of the "lighted district" of Madrid. We dropped our stuff off at the hotel and found ourselves smack in the middle of the shoe-shop area. Perfect.

I'm not much of a shopper. My preferred method is to know exactly what I want, go in the store, grab it if they have it, and leave. But I found the experience much more pleasant with Ben. He kept talking to me about what kind of boots he thought looked good on me, and he wasn't satisfied with going into just one shop (like me). He actually seemed to want me to look good and feel good about my purchase, and he wasn't just paying lip service to that notion. I felt a little special.

I didn't end up finding anything, but the fact that he was so interested and patient let me in on an intriguing side of Ben Anderson. I even commented on the nice scent of his new cologne. Mild, sweet, but strong . . . and a little mysterious.

Next, we were off to do a little pants shopping for Ben. Look, we are your typical dudes. Buying clothes lies somewhere on the bottom of my list of important things in my life. I have a family to think about: their schooling, their safety, the dogs, health insurance, the Seahawks, my next book to read, getting to a gym, and keeping up with baseball scores. They all rank way above shopping for clothes. I think

Ben is the same. But, man, he really needed a new pair of pants. His existing pair were not long for this world.

Black pants for tall, thin fellas can be hard to come by, as khakis and boxy jeans dominate the men's section of most stores. Finally, we happened upon a store that had promise. We noticed more of a "Euro" vibe with the cut of clothes and the clientele: lots of scarves, skinny jeans, V-neck T-shirts, and men dancing to Madonna.

Ben found a couple pair of pants his size and I followed him back to the changing area. I wanted to be as much help to him as he'd been to me in my boot search. He asked me if his butt looked good in the first pair that he tried on. "No," I said. "Too boxy." But the next pair was perfect. "Nice, Ben. Those pants give you a great butt."

He made his purchase as I got on the store Wi-Fi to check the MLB scores back home.

Our day off had a packed schedule. Once shopping was out of the way, it was time to hit the hotel gym and get a good workout in before our dinner reservation. Lucky for us, we discovered that we had the whole gym to ourselves. It's not uncommon to go without air conditioning in Europe, and we've learned how to deal with it. The sun had been beating down through the windows of this top-floor gym all day, and it was pretty much like a sauna. No problem.

On tour, you have to make a point of keeping your clothes clean. You can't just wear whatever you want at any time like at home. There isn't a washing machine everywhere you go. This is why you end up washing gym clothes in the hotel sink and hanging them to dry on your shower rod. The less clothes you have to dry, the less moisture you have in that bathroom, and the quicker whatever clothes you have in there will dry. Make sense?

This is a long way of explaining why Ben and I decided to go shirtless in the empty gym. A sweaty gym shirt would just be one more thing to wash and dry.

At the end of our rigorous workout, we did some assisted stretching. I helped him stretch, and he helped me. We were fairly soaked through with sweat, and Ben's hamstrings were really tight. I had him lie on his back, and I took his whole left leg and stretched it down toward him. Just then, a male hotel worker came through the gym, and his eyes got huge as he rushed uncomfortably and quickly past us. Weird.

Seeing as this was our first night off and that Ben and I were feeling rather civilized and refreshed from our cosmopolitan day, we both threw on the best clothes we had for dinner. I shaved, washed my hair, and used face moisturizing stuff. I put on my good-smelling cologne that makes me feel like part of the human race and dressed in my newer black stretch pants (with just a hint of a boot cut). I threw on a clean black Calvin Klein ribbed wifebeater, a black leather jacket, and a black scarf I had found, with just a wisp of silver (you know, to bring out the silver zipper of my jacket).

Madrid is known as the city of lights, and we were stunned by the overwhelming amount of light bulbs illuminating our walk to dinner. I imagine it is quite romantic.

The restaurant that Ben picked completely kicked ass—cloth napkins and cool art in a really old building in an ancient part of the city. After sitting down, we both ordered a different paella so that we could sample from each other. The customers were nice, and we kept getting smiles and little waves.

When it was time for dessert, we decided to order just one to split (you know, tour fitness and all). But it was so damn good, that we just had to order another to share. Afterward, we agreed that a long walk was in order to work off that extra dessert.

Our walk took us down the beautifully lit main shopping street of the Plaza Majore, ending down at the nineteenth-century Banco de Espana, which is still mostly gaslit, and a focal point for nighttime tourist photo ops. There was a group of college girls trying (and failing) to take a collective selfie. Ben, being the sweet dude that he is, offered to take the picture for them. This beautifully lit old bank building behind them was a grandiose backdrop, and it was clear why it is so popular with tourists at night.

When Ben got done snapping the photo on one of the girls' iPhones, they offered to take a photo of the two of us with the same backdrop. We posed for the shot, and one yelled: "Okay, put your arms around each other!"

Wait, what? What could possibly have given them the idea that we were a couple? Can't a couple of dudes walk off shared paella and dessert after a long day in one of the most romantic cities in the world without the smell of sex hanging in the air?

WHEN IN ROME . . .

"Life is tough, but it's tougher if you're stupid."
—JOHN WAYNE, *Sands of Iwo Jima*

SINCE I'M IN THE MIDST OF TELLING YOU ALL A STORY about a trip across the world, I want to give you all a few pointers that I've gleaned from my years spent on the road (and in the air). But, before I do, I want to make sure we're all on the same page. If you're going to be flying at all, there are some basics that those of us who do this for a living would love for you to check off your list.

Nobody wants to be "that guy." If you're not sure what to do these days with all of the extra security measures, do us all a favor and bone up a bit before you go. You look like a real dumb-dumb if you don't. Yes, we are all judging you as you make us wait longer in line, because you didn't take off your belt or shoes or didn't empty your pockets of change.

Yes, we are wondering what rock you just crawled out from under.

TSA and Customs and Immigration agents have become numb to the fact that we are all human beings with feelings, probably in the midst of a trip that we have been looking forward to for a while. I believe their numbness is a condition of simply dealing with an unbelievable amount of head-scratching dumbness. That, or they've been pretrained to think that when we step inside an airport we suddenly become the dumbest people who have ever walked the earth. Don't give them fodder that might add weight to their training.

Sure, we can be all punk rock and throw our thumbs at the man, but, look, there are some rules that should be followed. We're not kids anymore! Here are a few things you can do to help us all out:

Know the rules of where you're flying. Some countries have crazy rules. Before I flew to a gig in Dubai a while back, our manager sent us all an e-mail that said: NO MARIJUANA, NO COCAINE, NO PRESCRIPTION CODIENE, NO PRESCRIPTION VALIUM OR XANAX: ONE YEAR IN JAIL THEN DEPORTATION. Wow, OK, well, I've been clean and sober for a long time but still I think this through: "how 'bout deporting me first?!" Of course, the next line in the e-mail reminded me of a much larger problem, NO ISRAELI PASSPORTS OR ISRAELI STAMPS IN YOUR PASSPORT: INSTANT DEPORTATION. Really? Good to know, at least.

Empty your pockets. Yes, yes, by now everyone should know to take metal and questionable objects out of their pockets before they go through security. But it's amazing how many people don't! For those of you with an, um, checkered past, consider getting rid of some of those old pockets altogether. I ended up getting held in customs in Dubai for close to three hours. I started to panic. I thought, maybe they'd found some fifteen-year-old bindle of drugs lost in a dark recess of a coat pocket. It turned out to be nothing, and our passports were stamped and we were on our way. But there's a lesson here: because of this kind of paranoia and my history with substances that TSA frowns upon, I discarded all of my old luggage and most of my old (but KILLER) rock clothing when I got sober, for situations just like this. Now that pot is legal in a number of states—including my home state of Washington—the last thing you want is to find yourself on the wrong side of the law when you're flying to Phoenix. So give those pockets a deep clean, or get rid of them!

Leave something at home. Kind fellow traveler, please don't bring everything you have as carry-on. Of course that piece of luggage won't fit in the overhead bin. Now we must all wait while the flight attendants have to call the ground staff to put your shit underneath the plane. That's not inconvenient for the rest of us at all.

And when you bring all of that crap onboard, you do know to put it above your seat, right? How many times have I gone to my seat to find my overhead bin filled by someone who was just sick of carrying all of their shit down the aisle and apparently dumped it up in my space? Where the hell am I supposed to put my backpack? My legs are thirty-two feet long!

Be courteous. If it's a small plane, and the guy behind you is 6'3", don't be that guy who reclines the seat. You do feel the knees in your back, don't you? Think, man. Think!

In my twenties, when I saw the world for the first time, I behaved less like a traveler and more like a pirate, plundering about with my bandmates in search of treasure and booty. My experiences in some of the world's most beautiful places at the time consisted of visiting darkened bars, seedy alleyways, squats, and Italian tailors who didn't speak English but accepted American Express. (That's a book unto itself. In fact, it's called *It's So Easy (and other lies),* and it's out now in paperback.)

After I kicked the inebriates and found my wife, Susan, we put together our own band of travelers. Along with our two daughters, we've seen the world with our brothers in Velvet Revolver, Loaded, and Kings of Chaos. With small children, of course, you have to visit the places that they will enjoy. As a result, I could probably write a whole book on just places to take children when traveling (I'll call it *It's Not Easy (and I need a drink),* release date TBD).

Now that my children are teenagers, I'm back to traveling alone a lot (well, by alone, I mean the guys in my band)
or just with my wife. Now I make a point of visiting museums and historical sites or just going for a stroll (try that
with young kids!).

One of the first things I do when I travel to a new city
is try to discover what the locals do. I'm not too big on the
touristy-type of stuff. Tourist food and tourist factoids all
blend together into a homogenized stew of ersatz nachos
and cardboard hamburgers.

Here's a look at some of the knowledge I've absorbed
from a life spent on the road and a few tips for your next
journey.

KNOW YOUR WELSH IN WALES

Two of the three crew guys in this Walking Papers family
are Welshmen. The third guy, Paul, is from nearby Bristol,
England. The banter among the three of them is one-of-a-
kind hilarious. The Welshmen have something that the rest
of us never will: an understanding of writing and speaking
the Welsh language, which is very different and completely
unrecognizable from the English language.

The two Welshmen are Rob Jones and Jay Smith. These
dubious names should have tipped me off from the start.
I mean, Smith and Jones? Let's be real here. These last
names are made up. Probably a couple of stiffs on the run
from a bank robbery or something, now hiding out on a

rock tour. Rob and Jay can speak fluent Welsh, which, of course, gives them a sort of secret place to talk shit about the rest of us.

Bristol Paul, meanwhile, is no less shady. As I write this, he is sending me photos of sheep. This must be some sort of inside stuff that we 'Mericans don't get.

Since we'd played everywhere else on the planet except Rob and Jay's home country, it stands to reason that the last date on our previous run through the world was in Newport, Wales. Naturally, they were very excited to show us how cool their country is.

We arrived at a Holiday Inn–type of place about fifteen miles outside of the city the evening before the gig. This being the country and all, there wasn't a taxi service available to run us into town. We were hungry, and our only option was a pub across the motorway from the hotel.

Wales is famous for a few things that I know of: Tom Jones (of course), Princess Diana, Motörhead's Phil Campbell, Manic Street Preachers, Rob and Jay (natch), and Catherine Zeta Jones.

The pub was not unlike an American Black Angus or T.G.I. Friday's. There was a bar in the back, a "wait to be seated" area up front, booths and tables, and, of course, five guys who looked just like an age-appropriate version of Tom Jones. The food was perfect road fare: fries, chicken wings, a tuna niçoise salad, all served in those plastic red baskets with the paper lining. My takeaway from the evening was twofold: (1) this place really knows how to serve comfort food for the weary traveler, and (2) a lot of people in this area either really like Tom Jones, or I was at a gathering of Tom Jones impersonators.

The next day was gig day down in Newport, but, before I go further, let me explain something about a crew and band traveling together in the same bus: if one person needs one thing, no matter how big or small or trivial or unnecessary, everyone has to go. In the case of Newport, we needed 9-volt batteries. Rob and Jay decided to take us to the big grocery store just on the way into town. Not only could we get the batteries, but they had an espresso place inside and a deli. We'd all be able to get something to eat or whatever while we were there. Even better.

It became apparent why our Welshmen wanted to show this store off. It had everything. Bookstore? Sure. Luggage and bags? Of course. Footwear, gym shorts, and pants? Why not!? They also had an absolutely huge selection of food, which was great. But here's the thing, though: everything was in Welsh. The books, the labels, and those big signs in the aisles that tell you where to find, um, "products." I went in looking for a new microwave oven because the bus company asked us to replace our broken one.

Looking down the aisles at very fancy words I could only guess at, I began to feel like we were really in a foreign place. The language had stood the test of time and survived Roman conquering and Viking pillaging and Christian rule. I wondered where this exotic language originated: Surely some Greek, and perhaps a little Russian, and maybe some

Celtic? Just at that moment, I ran into Rob, and I began ex-
horting my theories about his language and its beginnings.

"Nah, mate," he said. "We just make words that sound
like the thing itself. Sure, we have taken some English into
account." He pointed to the deli aisle with the word "caws"
above it, "That's cheese, mate. And there (pointing to a sign
that spelled "grefi"), that is gravy!" Then he began to sound
out words that were taken from the sounds that the objects make. The word for a "rock," for instance, was a guttural and harsh-sounding use of consonants that did in fact
sound like a rock. Same thing for "air," "wind," and "fire."

When I asked Rob what the Welsh call a microwave, he
plainly stated, without the trace of a laugh or a joke, "Oh,
that's a popty ping." Right. Of course. Like the sound of pop-
corn popping in a microwave. He is totally fucking with me.

Newport has been around for a while and boasts a classic
village center that has grown outward over the centuries and
into this modern era. Old brick archways and Roman-era
stone bulkheads lead to cool antique stores and mediocre
Subway sandwich shops.

The Newport rock crowd is a serious affair. It's not a major metropolitan area, and this little neck of the woods often
gets passed over on the bigger rock tours. As a result, the
Newportians show up in force, and they are loud and joyous,
apparently a bit starved for rock. The Walking Papers had a
great show, and so did Alice in Chains, the evening's head-
liners. It was so good, in fact, that I had kind of forgotten
about the huge grocery store event from earlier in the day.

As I was getting ready to leave the venue, I wanted to warm some water for a cup of tea to go. There were a few venue staffers milling around, and I asked a young woman where the kitchen was. She saw my cup of water and correctly assumed that all I wanted was to warm it up. Pointing to a room situated next to us, she said, "Yes, but the popty ping is just in there."

Just when I thought I had Rob pegged.

DON'T EAT PEANUTS IN HARAJUKU

On a recent tour with Loaded, my daughters joined me in Tokyo for their first trip to Japan. They were super excited to go to an area in Tokyo called Harajuku (it has a trippy, hipster vibe). The day before they arrived, I decided to cab it over to Harajuku and do a little recon so that I could guide the fam through the maze with as much ease as possible. I have learned this recon tactic by getting lost with kids in tow too many times. Not cool or fun.

During the cab ride over, my stomach started to rebel from my questionable meal in Singapore the day before. This happens all the time on the road, and my cure-all (passed down from our road-dog forefathers in DOA and Black Flag—no shit) is salted peanuts. Upon my arrival in Harajuku, I ducked into a 7-Eleven-type of store and got a nice peanut-and-rice-cracker combo, perfect for eating and recon-ing on the go!

Harajuku is all connected by alleyways lined with themed shops in amazing contrast to each other: punk-rock clothes next to pastel-only skirt shops next to early-'80s NY beat-boy clothing next to a *Star Wars* store. It became obvious that many of the printed T-shirts with band names or *Star Wars* characters are bootlegs (last time I checked, Skywalker's first name is "Luke," not "Look").

It was in one of these alleyways that I stumbled upon a rock-and-roll (bootleg) T-shirt store. What caught my eye was a Metallica/GN'R split-band T-shirt in the front window. Of course, this shirt never existed in real life back in the day, but it got me to further peruse the inside of the store. I was met with a dazzling array of OG Guns N' Roses shirts with some "artwork" close to the original and other "artwork" comically missing. Just as I was looking at a skull-guys-on-the-cross GN'R shirt (where we all looked more like chimps than dastardly rock-and-roll hellions), I was asked to leave . . . for eating inside of the store.

I was relieved that they didn't recognize me. I rather hope that I look nothing like a skull-chimpy-type of rocker. Nope, I'm a rock-and-roll hellion, with salted peanuts on a mission to find the bunny-petting cafe and nail salon and *Alice in Wonderland*–themed restaurant in Harajuku.

I'm a badass.

HOLD ON TO YOUR WOMAN IN PARIS

Of course, everyone should try to get to Paris. The City of Lights really does ooze romance. The food and culture are second to none, and walking from the center of town to the

Place de la Republique, or strolling down the Avenue de la Grande-Armée, will fill all your senses and interests: art, food, people watching, angry cab drivers, and, at night, the lights.

The non-Français speaker must at least try to speak some French. You will be solidly rebuffed if the first words out of your mouth are "Do you speak English?" Through the years I've noticed that if you stumble through a few phrases and terms to a Parisian, they often become very helpful. If you don't at least try, you will get hosed.

That said, getting snubbed by Parisians is kind of funny. The amount of scorn some locals have for outsiders can be quite comical. On a recent tour, I went downstairs at the hotel looking for coffee a couple minutes after I woke up. In my best accent, I mustered up a "Café, s'il vous plait?" to the gentleman at the front desk. "Non!" he replied back rather gruffly, like I had just said something bad about his family. Ok. No problem. "Ou est le Starbucks?" I retorted. "I DON'T KNOWWWWW!" he said back to me totally loudly and with a weirdly abrasive and sneering tone. I've never quite figured out what his problem was. I just walked away.

One final tip for the fellas: the men here have no problem going after your wife right in front of you. Susan used to live in Paris and, thusly, speaks a bit of the local jargon. When she speaks French at a restaurant or bar, the men flock to mon amour. It's like I'm not even there.

WHEN IN FLORIDA, LOOK OUT FOR THE CITY COUNCIL

When you're traveling in a bus that is seventy feet long (with the trailer), it can be hard to find a good place to park.

One time Loaded's promoter got us permission to park in front of City Hall in a beach town suburb of the larger metropolitan Jacksonville. The problem with this was that a city council meeting was about to take place, and they were not alerted to our status as Very Important Parkers. My colleague Mike Squires and I were the only ones on the bus when we heard a knock on the door. A city councilwoman asked us who we were, and we politely explained our situation. She *seemed* OK with our answer and wished us a nice stay.

In actuality, she went straight into City Hall and brought out a bunch of her male council friends with the intent of getting us kicked off of the property. By this time, however, I was tired, hot, lonely, and a tad cranky. When one of the male council dweebs said in essence that I was lying about us having permission to park here, well, I kind of got in his face and asked him not to insult me any further and that I had been touring for more than half of my life and that we wouldn't do something as asinine as lying just to get a parking spot, especially in front of a shitty city hall. This guy was a real greasy and smarmy prick. He called the cops. Luckily, Squires knows how to handle the cops and an escalation of my righteousness was averted. But we had to move the bus. Fine.

That night, to celebrate being best friends and this being the longest I've ever been in a band with the same guys, we all got tattooed with some variation of the Loaded logo. The gig in Jacksonville kicked some serious ass, and that city council dude still has to deal with the fact that he has a small penis (OK, I guess that's one resentment that still needs working on). All was well.

MIX SEX AND TORTURE IN PRAGUE

GN'R played Prague in 1991 just after the Iron Curtain came down. It's interesting to see the changes here since then: gone are the drab Soviet-style colors, replaced by a rainbow of pastel and beauty. I highly recommend it.

When visiting this most beautiful of European cities, one has to take note that this place was unscathed during World War II. The spires of churches and castles here in Prague have been left pristine during our modern times of aerial warfare. So, definitely get out and walk the old part of the city. Go to the Charles Bridge, and follow the cobblestone path up to the castle tour (it took so long to build, eight hundred or so years, that this castle alone contains about twelve different architectural styles in it). Do the Haunted Prague tour, and go to the Torture Museum and the Sex Machine Museum. Pleasure and pain go hand in hand here in Prague.

Tip: Don't say "Hey! Are you Czechoslovakian?" here in the Czech Republic. There once was a united Czech and

Slovakia, but now they are two separate countries. You will get an evil stare if you make this slipup.

DRINK AND CRAWL IN DUBLIN

This Irish town has remained one of my favorite places on earth. The people here are friendly and love a good laugh, and the history of poverty and prosperity and shipping and potatoes will keep any tourist fascinated for days.

If you are a drinker, you have to experience a pub crawl. Every pub here has its own flavor and the Guinness is, of course, always on tap. In fact, the Guinness and Jameson whiskey factories offer tours. The center of Dublin has an electric nightlife, and the NOVA radio station plays great rock music.

But don't expect to understand anyone after about 10 p.m. The culture of hard drinking here is deeply ingrained. People like me who don't drink are looked at suspiciously, and I am often still offered a pint of Guinness, as if it doesn't count since I am in Dublin.

IN BELFAST, LEAVE YOUR TROUBLES BEHIND

When punk rock first reared its head, people were introduced to the genre through bands like the Ramones, the Dictators, and, later, the Stooges. The music was rough and impactful, but otherwise the songs were about cars, girls, fun, and dope.

In the UK and Ireland, though, there were political and class struggles that were pointed and scary. In America, we did not have the same level of economic problems that they had. And in America we had nothing close to imperialism intruding in on us.

When the Sex Pistols and the Clash records stormed into US record stores, we became educated on the seemingly exotic problems on their side of the water. Remember, there was no cable TV or World Wide Web. They definitely didn't teach us about the disgruntled working class in the UK or the Troubles in Ireland in school. Punk-rock music became much more than just a heavy riff with a snotty vocal.

There was a scrappy band from Ireland called Stiff Little Fingers whose songs told a rather bloody story about a people under siege. I had no idea at the time that the first two records—*Inflammable Material* and *Nobody's Heroes*—were personal stories of an area run red with blood: Belfast and Northern Ireland.

In 1980, I was fifteen years old, and, of course, lived at home. My mom was very supportive of me playing music, and she even pretended to take an interest in the Damned, the Jam, Germs, the Ruts, and whatever other records that I would play in our living room. She worked hard all day, every day. So when she got home from work, I would turn the volume down to give my poor ol' mother a break.

But I would sometimes see her looking through the jackets of the records I brought home. She wasn't looking for crude or inappropriate content. She was looking for common ground between the two of us. She was a nice and smart Irish lass with a huge curiosity for what was out there in the world.

One day, I came home from band practice and was surprised to hear the music of Stiff Little Fingers coming from the stereo. I knew it was not my older brother, Matt, playing my records, 'cause he was ONLY into jazz back then. As I entered our living room, I saw my mom holding the *Nobody's Heroes* jacket cover with tears streaming down her cheeks.

What I wasn't aware of until then was that my mom had been following the Troubles in Northern Ireland. It was where her father was from, and we had a lot of family living in and around those parts.

Political and, especially, religious strife had gotten that country into such a civil war of sorts that there was a fear-based gridlock choking the people as a whole. Terrorism and sabotage and car bombs were a daily occurrence for many years.

"Bloody Sunday," "Suspect Device" (the British term for a supposed bomb), and "Gotta Getaway" were just a few of the songs that suddenly came to life for me as my mother gently explained the intricacies of what these "poor boys" in Stiff Little Fingers must have been facing.

The Troubles are thankfully a thing of the past. Stiff Little Fingers are not. They are still alive and kicking some butt.

Tip: Tell someone "It's great to be in Northern Ireland." Take notice of the painted curbs in certain neighborhoods: the different colors used to delegate whether it was a Protestant or Catholic street.

VISIT CHECKPOINT CHARLIE IN BERLIN

I am a serious World War II buff, and just about everywhere you look in Berlin has had something to do with that world upheaval. The Allies split this city up back in 1946, and the Soviet side of Berlin, of course, started to close down communication to the point of building the famous Berlin Wall in 1961. For years, this city stood divided as an example of Western prosperity on one side and ruthless Soviet drab and paranoia on the other.

Tip: Visit the wall and count your blessings.

GET YOUR JAMBON IN BARCELONA

If architecture is your game, this is one of the most interesting cities to visit. The streets and buildings and parks teem with the touch of Antoni Gaudi, and the main cathedral (still being built 120 years later!) has four distinct sides that are amazingly different from the others.

Try to spend some time in the Gothic Quarter. But give yourself more than a couple hours to look around. The last time I was here, we arrived at something like 4 p.m. and had to quickly pull a full-on power-tourist move—hailing taxis and quickly looking at one sight before moving to the next—because we had a gig at 8 p.m. Also, try the jambon. Yes, it is just ham, but damn! They take pride in this locally produced meat staple.

TAKE LONDON OUT FOR A CHEAP DATE

This is probably my favorite city in the world outside of Seattle. London boasts every modern amenity while remaining a historical wonderland that one can get lost in forever. Transportation by subway (the Tube), bus, or train is impossibly easy. And a trip in one of their famous black taxi cabs is an absolute must.

I visited the city for the first time in 1987 when my brand-new band, Guns N' Roses, came to play the Marquee Club at the outset of the release of our first record, *Appetite for Destruction*. We had no money, but we had an apartment for two weeks in the Kensington area just off of Hyde Park. We had an absolute blast. You don't have to be a high roller to enjoy London. There is plenty to see that's cheap or free. Put the Natural History Museum and the Victoria and Albert Museum at the top of your list.

I have indeed been a high roller in London, too—or at least been around the highfalutin upper class. The private social clubs—often with an associated club in the country—is a peek into an age-old sort of caste system. The royals (dukes, earls, princes, ladies, sirs, and princesses . . . no shit) come to these clubs and so do the gilded upper class, actors, pop stars, bankers, and industrialists of every bent. Having dinner at one of these clubs one night with some friends who were members, I couldn't shake the feeling of a bygone era when the blue bloods (so named because of blue stains on their hands from handling too much silver) dined in these halls.

For everyday food, though, my favorite place is a chain called Pret A Manger. I know they have some shops in the States, but they started here, it's where I discovered them, and they'll always be a London destination for me. Pret has hot and cold wraps of all kinds (try the hot jalapeno chicken!), healthy sandwiches, great salads and soups, and strong espresso. This is always the first place I try to get to when I go to the UK, and they are on about every street corner in London. Cheap, fast, and kick-ass.

CONVERT DARKNESS INTO PRODUCTIVITY

THE SERENITY, RELAXATION, AND HUMANNESS I FELT in Madrid turned out to be a fleeting sensation.

After we played the gig, I came out of my euphoric fog and realized that I was still sick. Really sick. And getting worse.

Our next show was in Barcelona. Ideally, we would have hit the van immediately so we could rest up at our hotel halfway down the road. But our merch was still selling, and we couldn't leave it behind. So we stayed, knowing full well that our van would be parked in by Biffy's crew and we'd have to wait another four hours until they packed out and we could hit the road.

It was 1 a.m. before we made it out and 4 a.m. when we arrived at our hotel in Zaragoza, Spain.

When I'm on the road, I put my blinders on and focus on maintaining a fitness of body and mind. Without it, I can start to think about the dark. Darkness and I don't go well together. Working out in a gym, in a dojo, or backstage at an arena is the thing that cures me. When I'm this sick, the downtime can be a mental trick. That's why, instead of sleeping in, I got up early to sweat out the sick on a stationary bike.

For a few minutes, I was able to trick my brain and body into a state of being that shunned the sickness. On the way to the gig, I realized that the workout had made me much more ill.

To keep me above water in times like these, I employ a meditation that I learned early on in Ukidokan martial arts with Sensei Benny Urquidez. I've got a safe house in the meditation that I can build myself up from. One day I *will* be able to stretch my muscles and float above ground in meditation. I also know that there will come a day when my muscles won't propel me forward anymore, and this meditation will be all I have. For now, I'm grateful it can stave off the dark.

I used to spend a lot of time looking for drugs and drinking in bars or looking for bars with bathrooms in which to score drugs. Now, whether I'm on the road or at home, I try to put the time once reserved for darkness into healing my body and mind. To me, a workout is a reminder of my blessings: "I am lucky as hell to be here doing push-ups, jumping rope, lifting weights."

But I didn't lose a dependency. I merely exchanged one for another. If I miss a workout, I go through withdrawals. I hit the bag just as hard as I used to hit the drugs. Guys like me need something extreme to help center ourselves.

Finding gyms and temples of fitness becomes a sport unto itself when you're on the road. I've done yoga outside at 12,500 feet elevation in La Paz, Bolivia. I've found grand gyms with all new equipment in Hungary and Germany. I've worked out in fighter gyms with rusty weights in Birmingham, England. I've hit the bags in Fortaleza, Brazil, and Des Moines, Iowa. Years ago, I guess I'd have been bragging that "I did pharmaceutical cocaine in X location, and smoked some tar in . . . "

In English-speaking countries, it's easy to look up fitness centers, but the curvy and confusing lanes of England and Scotland make it almost impossible to find a gym.

One of my default moves is to just walk around town with a gym bag. I have no problem asking people on the street for directions. Wearing gym clothes and carrying a gym bag always seem to disarm people who would otherwise be a little freaked out by a tall, tattooed American walking in their direction. When I spot a local who's *also* wearing gym clothes—and, in the UK, you'll almost always spot someone coming from or going to a gym—I ask them if they can direct me to the same. Scoring a gym is no different than scoring dope: you look the part, ask for directions, and head to the right part of town.

Once, in Oxford, I woke up early on the tour bus, and, after fueling on coffee and packing my bag, I hit the streets. Sure enough, I spotted a fellow who looked like he had just come from a gym. Being the social guy that I am, I stopped him and asked if he knew where a walkable gym was. "Sure, mate," he said. "Just go down the road, take a left for a bit, then take a right, cross THAT road, and you will see a gate. There is a nice gym in there where all of the students work out at."

I must have just been concentrating too hard on this dude's directions to put two and two together. I took the left, and the right, crossed the road and, bam! There it was, Oxford's massive gym: Oxford University Sport. I guess the bloke did say something about students, didn't he?

I was convinced that there would be no way I would be allowed into the place. There, on a huge bronze plaque, was the inscription that Roger Bannister had first broken the four-minute mile (the very track was right there, to my right). I mean, this is OXFORD, for crying out loud! They don't let long-haired, tattooed stragglers like me just wander in, do they?

I meekly walked up to the receptionist, and, without much scrutiny at all, they said that for the equivalent of about US$9, I could get inside. Cool!

Inside, I was surrounded by athletes from the Oxford rowing club, the Oxford karate team, the rugby team, the football club, and, of course, the Oxford badminton team. I swore I saw an '80s version of Rob Lowe out of the corner of my eye.

Jet lag is a constant challenge for me. And there's nothing like a good workout to get you right after a long flight.

Once, after a brutal twenty-four-hour flight from Sydney to Dubai to London, I found a 9 a.m. Bikram yoga class. Landing at 6:30 a.m. at Heathrow, I knew I'd have to do something that would sweat out that flight. I'd heard that Bikram was sort of gnarly in this department, so I googled away and found a class that was relatively near my hotel.

By the time I got to the class, sleep deprivation was treating me to trails and noises that nobody around me had the pleasure of experiencing. As I got downstairs to the very hot room, a loud voice suddenly boomed into my frayed consciousness. *Welcome and namaste for making it here. The hard part is over. Just breathe.* Yeah. Really nice words—and I appreciate the gesture—but the yogi leading this class had a headset microphone attached to her, and the speakers were in like a 5.1 Sensurround configuration. Totally freaky.

She asked if there was anyone new to the class who hadn't done Bikram before, and I raised my hand from a face-flat lying position. "What is your name . . . name . . . name . . . name?" The speakers had some sort of delay on them, or I was really starting to trip. I'm not sure which one it was.

"Uh, my name is Duff."

"Welcome, Doug!"

"No. Uh, sorry, it's DUFF!" I said it a little louder in hopes that she'd catch it and we could move on.

"Jeff! Okay! Welcome, Jeff!"

Either way, I made it through the class, showered, and got about three cans of energy drink inside of me. Going to sleep in the middle of the day is a huge faux pas that will just lengthen your jet lag experience. Walk and drink energy drinks. Coffee will take you down. Take it from me. Stay up till 11 p.m. no matter what.

Gym etiquette is a learned skill that will be recognized in any language or locale. Keep your shit tight and your gym clothes clean. Bring a towel, and, to stave off an international incident, put deodorant on *before* you go to the gym, you damn animals. When I do cardio, I sweat like the proverbial whore in church. Sweating is fine and dandy in a gym, of course, but just clean up after yourself. This is appreciated in every time zone.

But even those who follow the aforementioned rules will be subjected to people who are just grumpy at life and find the gym a great place to exercise not only their body but also their grumpiness.

I once vacationed in a hotel in Hawaii that had a gym that was just steps from the beach. After a morning swim in the salty surf, I went to my room and changed for the gym. When I got to the gym, there was still some saltwater up my nose, and so I took a paper towel with me to an elliptical machine in case any saltwater was still left up my sinuses (we've all been there, right?). About fifteen minutes into my cardio workout, I wiped my nose as some water came out. I heard the guy on the machine next to me make guttural noises—I thought he was kicking ass on his cardio machine. A few minutes later, I wiped my nose again (don't forget, we are just steps from the saltwater, and the sound of people clearing their noses runs pretty much hand in hand with the beach). Again, the guy next to me started making noises again. As I looked over to make sure he was okay, he barked at me with a sharp German accent "YOU MUST KEEP YOUR NEIGHBORHOOD CLEAN!!!" My what?

This dude pointed at my paper towel, and said I must not come in with "ze flu!" I explained to him that I had just swam and that maybe he should chill the fuck out and that we were in Hawaii. "Just keep your neighborhood clean!!" was his only response.

Everyone has bad days. Some have bad days that turn into bad weeks and bad lives that cannot be cured when they're on the steps of heaven. When you encounter a situation such as this, leave it there. Never take that kind of stuff with you into your day.

As we progress through life, added peculiarities and challenges invariably arise along the way. Whether it's something physical, like tearing a meniscus in your knee or getting wrinkles on your face, to things of the mental nature, like depression or adult ADHD, having something physically wrong is seldom a thing to be publicly embarrassed about. *I gotta have shoulder surgery for a tear in my rotator cuff* is really not a big deal to expose to friends at lunch or to a stranger at the gym. But it remains taboo to talk about mental issues.

We are born with what we are born with. Some people have genetically strong shoulders and will never have a torn anything. Knees and teeth and receding hairlines are often predetermined. So, too, are mental issues.

I've dealt with something called panic disorder since I was sixteen years old. It came crashing down on me one morning at home while I was getting ready for school. I got into the shower, and suddenly the earth felt as if it had dropped down four feet. I thought it was an earthquake or that the foundation of my mom's house had crumbled. Then I started to sweat. I couldn't breathe. I yelled for my mom, and she got me to an emergency room as my breathing got shallower and my vision blurred intensely. I thought for sure I was curtains or that the LSD I had done at thirteen and fourteen was stored somewhere in my system and I would be stuck in a huge, nightmarish flashback.

When the doctor came into the room at the ER, he knew instantly that I was having a panic attack. What? I wasn't panicked about anything. After a nice dose of Valium, he sent me across the street to a psychologist who laid out the mental reasons that my brain would ignite into panic. He also cautioned that panic was a symptom of depression, or at least in the same family as depression. At the time, and for years to come, I would suffer many panic attacks, but nothing *near* depression. Hell, the panic attacks were *enough to handle!* And depression? Nah. Not me.

Over the years, a few of my good friends suffered from depression, and, in the course of trying to be a friend and be understanding, I'd listen and try to help. But I had no clue what depression was all about.

Then in 2012, my wife and I went to see the movie *The Iron Lady*. We went to one of our favorite art-house theaters in Seattle, and, as an armchair historian, the flick was right in my wheelhouse. I was sitting with my sweet wife, watching a good movie in a great theater. But halfway through the movie, my chair started to sink into the ground. My body became heavy. My thoughts suddenly darkened. This was not a panic attack. This was depression.

Where the hell did *this* come from? My life wasn't hectic or fucked up. My book had come out, I was in a good band, and my kids were doing great. No. I was terrified and really didn't know what was happening. We left the movie, and Susan called my boyhood friend Andy, who came over to the house and helped Susan talk me down.

I'm not the guy you'd peg for having bouts of depression. I generally look at the sunnier side of things and have learned to fight the good fight through life's ups and downs. What I'm finding out about this malaise, however, is that it has nothing to do with how my life is actually going at the time. It's a chemical malfunction in my brain that decides what it's going to do whenever it wants.

But this *has* to be looked at as an opportunity. I now have insight into something I really didn't know anything about, and now I can apply all of my martial arts training and long-distance bike and running training toward.

Once something like depression or panic rears its ugly head, the pathway is cleared for more episodes. I've had more of these bouts with depression. And, make no mistake, they are bouts. Fights. Knock-down and drag-me-the-fuck-down brawls. But it's something I'm up for.

I like to kickbox. I love to train very hard. Sensei Benny taught me how to train for fights. Fights can be long, and if you haven't trained to last twelve or fifteen rounds, you can get hurt. The way to train for that length of a fight is to remember that you must train harder than the guy you are fighting. *Always* train harder than the other guy. Whether it's a physical thing like boxing or a mental thing like depression, be the last guy out of the gym.

Depression wants you to stay still. It wants you to lie in bed. That's when you have to get up and run. If I am having black thoughts, I force myself up, and then I go and break a personal best record—or at least try. This has been my secret and savior. I run through it. I hot yoga with weights through it. I jump rope through it and lift weights through it. I write when I don't want to and ask my kids how school was and actually listen back through it. I make love through it and climb steep hills with a pack on my back through it.

I've got a weight on my chest and hope is trying to flee. My body is achy and heavy, and my neck hurts. This is my cue. *This* is the bell at the beginning of the fight. I put my running shorts and shoes on. *Lace up, motherfucker, it's time to move.* I smile and let the outside light in. *Let the light in.* Outside thoughts stay outside of my head. I stretch and drink water and plan my route. I run with my head up and my chest out and shoulders back. *"Be lighter than you are . . . "* Sensei Benny's voice rings in my ear. "Pick your feet up before they land, and be soundless. Be light. Be *light!"*

I pick up my pace and head for the stairs. I see people, and I send them all of my best thoughts. I run faster and leap up the stairs and do push-ups at the top and sprint, flat out, back to my route. I see another runner ahead of me, and I pace him, then pass him. I call these runners my angels. They pace me back to my light, and my chest heaves and my muscles strain and I break through.

As I reach the end of my run, I count down my strides, starting a half mile away at eight hundred steps. I know *these* eight hundred steps, and I also know they are bringing me home. Home. I also know that I have won this fight today. I have trained harder than the other guy. Today, the other guy was named Depression.

Running Workout
   —Stretch
   —Run 3.5 miles at an uncomfortable speed. Always
      push faster. Add sprints in the middle of your run.
      Stop and do push-ups and leg lunges every 1.2
      miles. Always end the run at your fastest.
   —Stretch

When I'm not on the road, one of my most therapeutic exercises is spending time in the ring.

Having balanced physical strength will bring more confidence and levity to your life. You will be more sure of your gait as you walk down the street. That confidence and endorphin release has the effect of letting the gluelike bad thoughts out of your system. Learning to box or doing some type of hard martial art will also make you lighter on your feet and put you in competitive face-to-face situations on a regular basis.

Sensei Benny calls the boxing ring the "square jungle." In this jungle there is opportunity to not only deal with your own fears and deep-seated angers but also to deal with the fears and angers of your opponent. Once you have your game together—your defense and cardio and footwork and combinations—your mind will begin to relax, and your confidence will take over. This square jungle is life. These are the same things you deal with outside of the gym. The ring is a gift to yourself and your opponent to work on the base necessities of being a better and happier human.

My first foray into the kickboxing ring was rather surreal. After working with Sensei Benny on a daily basis for ten months, he deemed me ready for the ring. I had trained physically and mentally and had sparred outside of the ring a bunch of times, but the ring was another level. If my sensei said I was ready, I too believed that I was ready. But my first real "opponent" was one Peter "Sugarfoot" Cunningham, a kickboxer who was training to retain his world middleweight championship. I was to be one of his many sparring partners.

When you train this hard, the ring is *everything*. How you *enter* the ring should be an extension of your persona and confidence. But me being 6'3" and 160 lbs., I *can* look awkward if I let myself. The last thing I wanted to do was trip over a rope or come in on my knees. Seriously, if you've never gone through the ropes and you have a world champion waiting for you . . . it's kind of a big obstacle. But I had the confidence of my sensei, and by this time I finally had good footwork, too. This would be no problem. Of course, I stumbled on the first rope and went too high on the second rope. It probably looked like Jerry Lewis was entering the ring.

Sugarfoot wasn't there to play. He didn't know or care that this was the first time I was in a kickboxing ring. He was dead serious about getting ready for this fight. I was simply a tool with which he could work. It quickly became obvious to me that "ring cardio" is different from any other type of cardio. My sensei yelled for me to relax my shoulders and keep my hands up: "Jab and *move!* Double jab! Triple jab! *MOVE!*" It also became obvious that Peter Cunningham was working on his axe kicks.

An axe kick is when a very flexible and strong person brings his leg straight up and a bit to the side and lowers his heel at a high rate of speed onto his opponent's shoulder, nose, or upper pectoral muscle. The result is pretty much a nonuse of the area that has been stricken by said heel. It's a lethal offensive move, for sure.

The thing about an axe kick from a guy like Sugarfoot is that you don't see it coming. Since it was my first time sparring, my eyes hadn't been trained for what to look for. *BOOM!* I got a fierce axe kick to my left shoulder, and suddenly my left arm felt paralyzed. My left jab was gone. I changed my stance to southpaw (something we worked on a lot), but then another axe kick to my right shoulder took out my jab from that side. Every time I'd front kick Cunningham to keep some space, he would thigh kick my supporting leg. When I tried front kicking with the other leg, he'd just thigh kick the other supporting leg—all the while peppering my now defenseless face with jabs and right crosses. I'm afraid that I didn't give him much of a contest. But I did last the three rounds I was scheduled to be in there.

After the bell rang on that third round, Sugarfoot came up and told me that I did a good job. He also said that I could tell my friends that I "lasted three rounds with the world champion." I will never, ever forget that. Sixteen months prior I had been in the ICU with a burst pancreas. This was victory indeed.

Those first few years in the kickboxing gym showed me how to live a new life. This life now includes not gentle workouts but full-on strenuous conditioning sessions. In the dojo, you don't want to stop training, because the guy who trains harder than you is going to be the guy you meet in the ring.

Always train harder than the other guy.

Always keep your neighborhood clean.

Kickboxing Workout

—Wrap hands

—3 minutes jump rope and 1 minute rest while doing push-ups (5 sets)

—3 sets of 20 hanging abs

—50 burpees

—Stretch hamstrings, quads, back, neck, glutes, calves, ankles, and shoulders

—3-minute rounds of each of the following:

   -Jab bag

   -Combination (jab, right cross, left hook, etc.)

   -Front and side kick

   -Body bag (hands)

   -Thigh kicks, round kicks, axe kicks, and donkey kicks

   -Flying kicks

-Knees and elbows

-Gap bag (close distances with combinations of
hands, feet, elbows, and knees)

—Spar with a partner for 3 to 5 rounds (Wear mouth-
piece and cup—if you're a guy. Actually, women
should wear mouthpieces and a cup, too.)

—Shadowbox to cool down

—10 minutes of slow jump rope

Gym Workout

—30 minutes of cardio (20 minutes at maximum heart
rate, 10 minutes at 70 percent). Do cardio before or
after weights.

—3 sets of 25 push-ups (or max), interspersed with 3
sets of abs

—Stretch

—3 sets of pull-downs, interspersed with 3 sets (20) of
front flies

—3 sets of 15 lunges, each leg

—2 sets of calf raises with a weight in hand. Follow calf
raises with one-legged jumping on the ball of that
foot.

—3 sets of hamstring curls

—3 sets of 15 Superman back crunches

—3 sets of 20 curls, interspersed with 3 sets of triceps

—Finish with 50 burpees if you started with cardio

SKIP THE STRIP CLUB, HIT THE BOOKSTORE

THE FIRST TIME I TOURED THIS REGION IN MY TWENTIES, I can guarantee you that finding a local bookstore was not on my itinerary. I had fleshier locales on my mind. These days, bookstores take up the space in my life once reserved for bars and strip clubs. I'm like a kid in a candy store when facing shelves and shelves of books. The only poles at these places hold up bookshelves, and the only crack is the small sound a book makes when it's opened.

I do pretty much all of my reading on a Kindle, but I buy the physical books, too. That is, I buy the e-book for my device and the hard cover for my bookshelves. The Kindle isn't always the best way to find new books. It's cool, for sure, in that you can instantly download books that you read about or are referred to—and it's so much easier to bring a Kindle on the road than a backpack full of books. But a bookstore is the ultimate way to immerse yourself in what's new. You can browse, and you can ask around, something you can't do as well in the cocoon of e-commerce.

It can be the littlest hint or clue that sends people looking for a book and thrusts their life briefly in new directions. It can be gossip you hear in line for an espresso or a movie you see on espionage. The direction of your reading can very well influence your life for a while.

I'm not much for Hallmark bromides, but a friend sent me a card once that infected my headspace for months. The front featured a quote from Ralph Waldo Emerson, an author I had yet to be exposed to:

> Finish each day and be done with it. You have done what you could. Some blunders and absurdities no doubt crept in; forget them as soon as you can. Tomorrow is a new day. You shall begin it serenely and with too high a spirit to be encumbered with your old nonsense.

I reread it about twenty-eight times over the next few days and became enchanted with this Emerson dude. How did he know I needed to hear this? How did he know we all need this kick in the ass sometimes? What else does he have to say?

A recent study reported that 30 percent of men don't read a book every year. If you've gotten this far, you are already ahead of a large percentage of your class. If you're wondering where to turn to next, here's a list of some of my favorite books that have kept me company at home, on the road, and backstage:

Stephen Ambrose, *Undaunted Courage*: Ambrose is most famous for his book *Band of Brothers*, which was turned into the epic HBO miniseries of the same name. Ambrose was a prolific history writer whose interests and expertise were wide. *Undaunted Courage* unravels the journals of the Lewis and Clark expedition—the uncharted exploration of US-owned parts of North America circa 1805. Read it and you'll be reminded why Ambrose is considered one of the best writers of American history.

Jack Black, *You Can't Win*: My good friend and Loaded bandmate, Mike Squires, found me this page-turner in Portland's famous Powell's Books. *You Can't Win* was reportedly William S. Burroughs's favorite book and a cornerstone of his writing style. The edition I own includes an introduction by Burroughs himself. The book follows Black's rough-and-tumble childhood that eventually brought him to a life of crime, riding the trains while crisscrossing the United States at the turn of the century. Black tells an uncompromising tale of his absolute fascination with the life of a "yegg" (a homeless vagrant who chose a life free of the 9-to-5). The book is really quite fascinating in that Black's voice throughout the book stays true to the parlance of the 1920s.

Jon Clinch, *Finn:* This book is a Cormac McCarthy–esque look at a fella named Finn; a bedraggled and alcoholic man who fathers a son with a runaway slave in Illinois in the 1850s. His son's name is Huckleberry and, yes, this is the preceding story we all know, told through Clinch's eyes. This is a brilliant—if dark—take on what happened in Huckleberry Finn's early life.

Steve Coll, *Ghost Wars: The Secret History of the CIA, Afghanistan, and Bin Laden, from the Soviet Invasion to September 10, 2001:* Al Qaeda, counter-terrorism, government fuckups, and all the rest. *Ghost Wars* won the Pulitzer Prize in 2005, and although it's easy to dismiss book awards, I've found that when it comes to nonfiction, the Pulitzer stamp is to be respected. I'm sure that Coll must have had a ton of help in sorting through the mind-numbing amount of documents and whatnot that he used to write this book. The question is, How did he make it all so readable?

Edward Dolnick, *Down the Great Unknown:* This is the epic true story of adventurer John Wesley Powell and his journey down the Colorado River. The year 1862 saw the end of the Civil War and gave birth to a whole slew of young men who wanted to see the beauty in life after so much horror. A British friend suggested this book. Sometimes it takes that outside fascination with your own country's history to light a spark.

Jennifer Egan, *Black Box*: Egan's first piece of fiction since *A Visit from the Goon Squad* furthered my belief that she is one of the best and most forward-thinking fiction writers of our generation. She is punk rock and cosmopolitan and inventive. *Black Box* originally came out on Twitter via @NyerFiction. The limited-edition bound proof copy that I own has a permanent place on my bookshelf of greatness.

Jennifer Egan, *A Visit from the Goon Squad*: This Pulitzer Prize–winning piece of fiction is about punk rock, self-destruction, and redemption. Wait . . . I know that story.

Timothy Egan, *Short Nights of the Shadow Catcher: The Epic Life and Immortal Photographs of Edward Curtis*: This National Book Award–winning book by a writer from my hometown, Seattle, is a page-turning look at treasured and celebrated photographer and ethnographer of Native American culture, Edward Curtis. If you are already a fan of Egan's writing style, then you will know of his gripping and fluid prose. We will all instantly recognize many of Curtis's early and beautiful "Indian" photos. This is the story of how hard Curtis worked to get these shots, and how head-over-heels in love he fell for the plight, wisdom, religion, language, and people of the many, many indigenous tribes scattered throughout the American West, Canada, and the

Arctic. Curtis sacrificed his family and livelihood to pursue what he saw as a life's work: to preserve and archive what was left of the quickly disappearing customs and people who were in North America first. This is an instant Egan classic.

Timothy Egan, *The Big Burn*: As that "radical," President Teddy Roosevelt, was nationalizing huge swaths of our US forests and trying to stock them with a few good men and women (the first forest rangers) to protect the trees from evil clear-cutting lumber companies, a massive fire-fueled anomaly of a hurricane swept through the inland Northwest. The year was 1910, and there was no such thing as forest firefighters yet. The saga that ensues is an edge-of-the-chair feat of death, survival, heroics, and frustration. This book makes me want to take a driving tour of eastern Washington, Idaho, Montana, and Wyoming, just to see the remnants of the 110-year-old megafire.

Timothy Egan, *Breaking Blue*: Spokane, Washington, was once a burgeoning promised land of wealth and growth. During the American dust bowl and Depression, Spokane became a main destination for people looking to start anew. But Spokane was also a place run with an iron fist by the law, where graft, prostitution, liquor running, and burglary were all reserved for the police. If you stepped in the way of any of these vices, you may have gotten killed . . . even if you were another cop.

Ralph Waldo Emerson, *Self-Reliance* (Essay): Some of us have religion and faith, while others look for spirituality elsewhere. Many have faith in science and logic. Some of us have simple love from our family, and others have nothing at all. For those of us always searching and open to ideas, consider this essay. Like the above quote, *Self-Reliance* is a rereadable meditation on the innate feelings of victory and perseverance that we all have at our fingertips. You're welcome!

Dexter Filkins, *The Forever War*: I wear my friends out recommending this one. But, look, it becomes their favorite, too, so I can't stop! Iraq and Afghanistan are two big clusterfucks that have so many peoples' lives on the line. We should all be as best informed as we can. *The Forever War* gives a view with scope and honesty.

F. Scott Fitzgerald, *The Great Gatsby*: I guess there is a reason they call it a classic. This is perfect fiction. I never took the chance to read Gatsby during my abbreviated high school career. If you, too, missed it while you were starting rock bands, give it a look. It's pure joy to read. Fun fact: Hunter S. Thompson typed every word in this book just to get the feel of writing perfect fiction.

Michael Finkel, *Here Be Monsters* **...** *50 Days Adrift at Sea* **(Kindle Single):** I couldn't tell you why, but I enjoy stories of survival and misery. This is one such story. Three fifteen-year-old boys from the tiny speck of the island nation called Atafu in the South Pacific got drunk and decided that they had had enough of living so far away from the modern world. They made the inebriated, knee-jerk decision to steal an uncle's fishing skiff and set off on an adventure. There was no other land anywhere nearby. They did not bring any water or food. They guessed that they'd probably be found within a day or two. They were not. The boys did survive their fifty-eight-day ordeal, but just. Finkel does an outstanding job of reportage here.

Thomas Friedman, *The World Is Flat: A Brief History of the 21st Century:* Don't let the nonfiction-ness of this book's title throw you off. *The World Is Flat* is, like all of Friedman's books and columns, immensely readable, informative, well-rounded (for a nonprimary source especially), and just plain outstanding. If you want to be informed on what is up with globalization and digitalization topics, get you some of this book.

Heimlich Harrer, *The White Spider:* Movie viewers are familiar with Harrer through Brad Pitt's portrayal of him in *Seven Years in Tibet.* Did you know that this amazing man (Harrer, not Pitt, ladies) took part in the first successful climb of the north face of the Eiger in 1938? This book will leave you gasping.

Laura Hillenbrand, *Unbroken*: *A World War II Story of Survival, Resilience and Redemption*: I read this book when it came out in 2010 and immediately recognized it as the best piece of nonfiction I had read in years. If you haven't read it yet, just go do it now. It's a fascinating story of an Olympic runner who found himself shot down in the Pacific and a prisoner of the Japanese. An epic adventure.

Adam Hochschild, *King Leopold's Ghost*: Hochschild is, in my opinion, one of the most readable and well-researched nonfiction writers of our time. This is THE ultimate story of colonization of Africa, with Belgium giving no thought whatsoever to the genocidal effects their endeavors had on the human beings of the Congo.

Michael Hodgins, *Reluctant Warrior*: Just when I thought I had read everything worth reading about the Vietnam war, boom!, out comes another great account. Michael Hodgins writes with ease about his time as a Marine at the end of the war.

Kazuo Ishiguro, *Never Let Me Go*: I know that there are some pretty pointed opinions when it comes to this author and this book. Ishiguro—like Cormac McCarthy—is an author people either love or hate. Like McCarthy's *The Road, Never Let Me Go* is not so much about the story itself but how it is told, the relationship between characters, and the usage and turns of a phrase. If you like to go to dark places, give this book a try. If you like butterflies, unicorns, and rainbows, well, stay far, far away.

Sebastian Junger, *War*: This book is a written account of Junger's time spent at a forward fire base (Restrepo) in Afghanistan, and is a companion to *Restrepo,* the documentary he made with photojournalist Tim Hetherington (also a must). Where the documentary simply lets the film tell the story, Junger's book fills in the gaps. Junger has become a master storyteller, both in researched topics (*The Perfect Storm, A Death in Belmont*) and in his firsthand accounts of war. The line between journalist and combatant has fully been blurred with the advent of IEDs (roadside bombs). Whereas a journalist can be snarky and full of politics in the rear, the frontline journo like Junger seems to have a much more human and apolitical directive. The motto seems to be: "Survive Today and Write the Truth Without Doing Harm to Those Who Protect You That Day." Junger did a very honorable job here. Neither pro- nor antiwar, just a day-to-day account of some young men in extreme danger.

Steven Kasher, *Max's Kansas City: Art, Glamour, Rock and Roll*: This is one of those coffee table books that a guy with my influences just has to have. I didn't get it on my birthday, but purchasing a book like this feels celebratory. I never got to go to this club in New York before it closed down, but if you are a fan of the Ramones, the New York Dolls, Iggy Pop, Bruce Springsteen, or Patti Smith, then you undoubtedly know of the lore of this hallowed ground.

Michael Korda, *With Wings Like Eagles: The History of the Battle of Britain:* This is a book that I read while touring the UK and Ireland. It is always insightful for me to try to read a historical book on places that I am visiting. War history, for me, is much more than the study of conflict; it is also an insight into how people coped and lived and suffered and triumphed in extraordinary settings. Korda's *Battle of Britain* illuminates the strategy and players involved in the buildup to this turning-point battle against Hitler and the Luftwaffe. It's completely fascinating.

Jon Krakauer, *Into Thin Air:* This 1997 masterpiece sparked a fervor that drove me to read about cold, scary places high in the air.

Peter Krass, *Carnegie:* If you are a lover of history and the big and beefy earth-moving characters that shaped much of it, get this tome. It's a massive but amazingly readable and enjoyable undertaking.

John D. Lukacs, *Escape from Davao*: I've read a shit-ton of books about World War II and have spent a lot of that time zeroing in on things in the Pacific. The Bataan Death March, and anything to do with being a prisoner of the Japanese, is right in my wheelhouse. This story of Airman Ed Dyess's escape from a Japanese labor camp in the Philippines is as epic as *Unbroken*. Lukacs, a top-notch nonfiction writer, pulls the facts of warfare, distance, hunger, and fear into a fully engaging read.

Cormac McCarthy, *Blood Meridian*: OK, get comfy, because I'm gonna start talking about Cormac McCarthy. As I've already made clear, I'm a big fan of the prose and rhythm of Mr. McCarthy's writing. *Blood Meridian* takes the reader through a relentless, bloody campaign of revenge between a Mexican Army/US Calvary mash-up of figures and the Comanche band they are after. This is a book for men!

Cormac McCarthy, *Outer Dark*: Yep. Another dark and twisted look into the American soul. Poverty. Misery. Suffering. Loss. Nothing like a little Cormac fiction to put a little spring in your step. Genius!

Christopher Moore, *Lamb*: If you like Jesus and adventure and kung fu and hookers, please read *Lamb*. If you have no sense of humor and follow religion blindly, this book may not be for you. As a student of theology at a fine Jesuit university in Seattle, I found *Lamb* to be brilliant, well-informed, and funny as hell.

Andrew Nagorski, *The Greatest Battle*: Nagorski has become the ultimate World War II historian since the passing of Stephen Ambrose, and his writing will send you to the footnotes looking for more books on war (Nagorski's reference material has now become my de facto reading list). A lot of us think of the battle for Stalingrad as the big turning point of the Soviet/German conflict in World War II. Nagorski takes us through the (for some reason) little-told story of Hitler's army getting to the city limits of Moscow and the great lengths that Stalin went to to save his city. It is amazing to think of the insanity of Stalin and Hitler and how so very recent in history this was. This is a must-read for any war/history buff.

Andrew Nagorski, *Hitlerland*: Another World War II instant classic from Nagorski. Here, he illustrates the unlikely rise of the Third Reich through the eyes of American journalists who reported on Germany from 1921 to 1941. It's a fascinating and thought-provoking angle.

Miklos Nyiszli, *Auschwitz*: A terrifying eyewitness account of the most diabolical human horrors. Dr. Nyiszli wrote of his horrible experience just as the war ended. He survived for twelve months in the concentration camp by keeping his mind focused on science. This book is brutal, but for the historian and those fascinated with how far human evil can go in real life, it is essential.

Tim O'Brien, *The Things They Carried*: This may be the most poignant book ever written about the US involvement in Vietnam. O'Brien was a nineteen-year-old kid when he went to Vietnam as an Army enlistee with a huge talent for writing and observation—and a fear of dying in the field.

Michael B. Oren, *Power, Faith, and Fantasy: America in the Middle East, 1776 to Present*: If you are interested in America's involvement in the Middle East—the whos, whys, and how-the-hells—then this book is a great all-in companion to Thomas Friedman or Steve Coll. Author Michael B. Oren is as good as David McCullough when it comes to making nonfiction read like an epic, page-turning novel.

Donald Ray Pollock, *The Devil All of the Time*: Pollock is a master. I was unfamiliar with his work until a friend who owns a hip, independent bookstore in the Bay Area gave me the heads-up. If you are from somewhere around Knockemstiff, Ohio, you may find this book too close to home. But for a good ol' peek inside of the underbelly of America, try anything by Pollock.

Donald Ray Pollock, *Knockemstiff*: Once you start, you cannot stop reading Pollock. Knockemstiff, Ohio, is, according to Pollock's storytelling, a desperate, no-win corner of America. In the same sense that Cormac Mc-Carthy can make a reader queasy with the necrophiliac in *Children of God*, Pollock can do the same with his speed-sniffing, glue-huffing ruffians and sex fiends.

Andres Resendez, *A Land So Strange: The Epic Journey of Cabeza de Vaca*: I love these kinds of books. The subtitle says it all: "The Extraordinary Tale of a Shipwrecked Spaniard Who Walked Across America in the 16th Century." Now THAT is what I call a real story!

William L. Shirer, *The Rise and Fall of the Third Reich: A History of Nazi Germany*: I wanted to read this from the moment I finished Nagorski's *Hitlerland*, which documented how bellicose toward Hitler one journalist was: William Shirer. The breadth, scope, detail, and research that Shirer pours into this book is absolutely second to none. Shirer was in Germany as Hitler took over. He stayed there and reported to the rest of the world until 1941 when America entered the war (and he was kicked out). Shirer came back for the Nuremberg Trials and combed through tons of captured Nazi and Wehrmacht documents, as well as confiscated personal diaries of many of the top German military and Nazi party brass. That Shirer could assimilate all of this material and make it such a readable story is really beyond comprehension.

Upton Sinclair, *The Jungle*: A lot of you probably already read this in your senior year of high school. But I didn't have a senior year in high school and, thus, didn't read Sinclair until just a couple of years ago. The man's a genius. *The Jungle* is one of the darkest accounts we have of industrial Chicago in the early twentieth century. It'll make you think twice before you eat another hot dog!

Upton Sinclair, *King Coal*: Again, Upton takes a deep, eye-opening look into industry and exposes all of the wrongs and class warfare between the haves and have-nots. Few authors have done as much as Sinclair to exert pressure to change our modern view of work conditions and inequalities. He does it all in the rubric of a page turner. Stunning.

Upton Sinclair, *The Moneychangers*: I'm not sure what the difference is between Goldman Sachs selling financial vehicles that are built to fail and Sinclair's 1910 Northern Mississippi Railroad stock being sold to a public that had no idea of the bad intentions of its chairmen. *The Jungle* did much to change child-labor laws and food-inspection laws. I wonder why Wall Street wasn't put on a tighter leash after it was exposed by *The*

Moneychangers? This hundred-year-old book is suddenly very topical and relevant.

Corey Taylor, *Seven Deadly Sins*: I've known Corey (of Slipknot fame) on a personal level for the last few years and have come to know him as one of the smartest dudes out there. When he told me about his foray into writing, I had no doubt that whatever topic he chose to write about would be deep and heavy. *Seven Deadly Sins* is a funny yet poignant look at Corey's dip into drugs and vice and asinine behavior in his youth. But it also studies the age-old question of whether certain personal traits are learned or bred into a person. Corey is one of those people who just seems impossibly good at whatever he chooses to pursue. I have no doubt that this tome will reflect this fact to you, too.

Rachel Trezise, *Dial M for Merthyr*: This is one of those books that when it spills out of my backpack at the airport or backstage, people in the know around me give me an enthusiastic thumbs-up. This is a rock-and-roll book, and it is a social study done in real time, about a young rock band from Wales and a young writer in the back of their tour bus taking notes.

Paul Trynka, *Iggy Pop: Open Up and Bleed*: If you lean more toward rock and roll and if you are a Stooges, Iggy Pop, or even David Bowie fan, *Open Up and Bleed* is the most complete and well-researched book you're gonna find (and there have been a few)—and not just on the Stooges. Trynka's got the goods on how Iggy got the name Pop, the downfall and return of Iggy's solo career, and finally the triumphant return of the Stooges. I read this book on tour and it inspired some good rock moments onstage, for sure.

BE LOYAL

W HEN I'M ON THE ROAD, SKYPE, E-MAIL, AND CELL phones are what keep me in touch with my family and allow me to juggle the half-dozen projects I have going on at any given time. And I admit that I don't know where I'd be without them. But electronics don't run my life.

As a grown-ass man of this modern age, I believe there are certain things we must do—and should not do—to retain some dignity in this time of social media jibber-jabber and Insta-everything. Yeah, I've got a Twitter account, but I don't update it every time I pass by an ironic T-shirt. Sure, I take pictures on my phone once in a while, but I'd rather *live* in the great moments of my life than make sure that I get a picture of them.

I think iPhones are swell and fine, especially for my teenagers. Around 2006, I finally submitted to our era and stepped up from a simple fold-top cell phone to a Black-Berry. At first, it seemed like a lot to handle. The fact that I could receive e-mails to my phone was a bit too convenient. I felt too available. Remember before smartphones when you couldn't really check your e-mails until you got Wi-Fi on your laptop out on the road or got home to your computer?

As I started to write weekly columns for *Playboy, Seattle Weekly,* and ESPN, I found the keyboard on the BlackBerry to be a godsend. Out on tour, I'd often write my columns from my trusty BlackBerry and send them off straight from there. I started to hear from my editors: "You wrote this on your *BlackBerry?!*" How did you know? Is it really that bad? "No! It says 'Sent from my BlackBerry' on the signature!" OH!

My BlackBerry became an extension of my thought processes. To write, a person has to be comfortable with whatever medium they write with, and my trusty BlackBerry became a safe place for me to express myself.

That was good enough. It did everything I wanted it to do. My BlackBerry probably doesn't do everything that *your* smartphone does. And if it does, I don't want to know about it. A BlackBerry is for business. For my business, it's a place to check and respond to e-mails, post my gig dates through Twitter, and write my columns.

A gentleman of this modern age doesn't play video games on his gadget nor stay glued to social media on his gadget. In fact, a gentleman of this modern age should really stay away from social media (unless you follow @DadBoner or @HenryRollins on Twitter, of course).

As iPhones and Androids came along and began to absolutely dominate the market, I started to get looked at with a bit of amusement when I pulled the old BlackBerry out of my coat pocket. "You *still* have a BlackBerry?!!" the kids would say. Yeah. Yes I do. I'm doing business, and I don't play games out here in the real world. Didn't you notice that when North Korea took down Sony Pictures, the company went back to their BlackBerries? They knew where to turn for safety, security, to get it done.

I stand up for my gadget and am constantly amazed by iPhone snobbery. But, really, this just speaks to how we deal with loyalty.

I'm a loyal motherfucker. I know a bunch of us are. Whether it's OG punk rock or rap, Calvin Klein briefs, Pennzoil, or the girl that we love, there are men of this modern age who insist on loyalty.

No band was better than the Damned in 1977 or the Clash in 1978 or Ice T on the *Power* record. Period. *My War* and *Damaged* are necessary Black Flag records. You get what I'm saying here? That's loyalty.

Loyal people grew up with a good dog. Loyal people have a mom they think is a saint. Loyal people get disappointed when others break their trust. Loyal people stay with their BlackBerry. Forever. Or at least until the company stops making them.

I run into guys my age who, like me, were part of the first wave of American punk rock. It was a risky time to be dressing punk, and there were many times we got into fights or got straight beaten up by gangs of jocks who thought we punkers should be taught a lesson. Because we were into something we thought was the most forward-thinking medium, we could see the folly in closed-mindedness and learned to adapt and to *protect* our punk-rock music. We were loyal to the bands, and we were loyal to each other. To this day, there is still an allegiance felt between us old-school punker dudes.

I think a lot of how I am loyal to things these days is totally informed from those punk-rock days.

The BlackBerry is a rare species to spot in the wild these days, but it's out there. We BlackBerry users know who each other are, and I sense a whiff of dignified air when we cross paths. We nod knowingly. BlackBerry owners are the ones taking care of all of the real business that makes our world go around. And we know it.

Pilots tip their hats to us as we get on planes. Bank managers rush out of their offices to greet us. Bartenders send us free drinks. Restaurant owners give us the best tables.

You all wouldn't know this stuff. You're too busy posting to Instagram, while we're busy getting it done.

GET A DOG

I MISS MY GIRLS.

Diarrhea has set in. I've had to sneak into the bathroom of the diner across the street about a dozen times.

I miss Susan. Being apart doesn't get easier. It's worse when I'm sick. I have a fever. There's no time to visit the doctor. We have to be in Paris tomorrow.

I miss Grace and Mae. It hurts to think of them at home, without me, getting a head start on Christmas.

I miss my dogs. Sure, they destroy the furniture and take up the entire bed, and I have to apologize in public for my farting pug. But my dogs are part of what makes our house a home.

A dog named Chloe helped me become a better man.

To me, the parallels of the *Marley and Me* story to my life are almost uncanny. I've written a weekly column, as did John

Grogan, the author of *Marley and Me*. Chloe was a naughty and mischievous girl in her youth, as was Marley. Chloe chewed up anything and everything . . . so did Marley.

Chloe helped us raise our daughters and would know beforehand when one of them was going to be sick or otherwise out of tilt. Chloe would help nurse them back to health without expectation of reward. Chloe loved us without condition, and she became the love of our lives.

When she got sick with liver cancer at the age of thirteen, we nursed her back and did everything we could to ease her pain. When the stairs at our house became too much of a hurdle for my girl, I would carry her up so that she could sleep with us, her family.

When we brought our first baby home from the hospital, we had no idea what to expect from Chloe. Until then, she had sort of ruled the roost, as it were, as our only child. Chloe had previous experience in motherhood. As a one-year-old young lass before she got spayed, she snuck out of the house and got knocked up. A few months later, she had a record FOURTEEN puppies!!! It was one of the happiest times in my life having all of those little guys in my house, and Chloe tirelessly handled her motherly duties like a pro. A few years later, as we brought our new infant home, Chloe instantly knew that her role in the family had changed. She slept underneath Grace's crib every night and gently played ball with her as she grew.

When we had our second daughter, Chloe accepted her duties without question or forlorn, but she did start to tire more easily. In return, my girls let her rest when she needed it, and they got an early sense of responsibility. They seemed to sense that Chloe now needed *them* too.

When it came time to put Chloe down, my wife and I bawled as we loaded her into the back of my Ford Bronco. I called my English professor at Seattle University to tell him that I would not be able to make class that day, and he heard the pain in my voice. Professor Sam Greene was a visiting poet, and I was fortunate enough to get into his class. As I told him the reason for my absence, he began to cry right along with me over the phone. I will never forget that.

Just before the vet put the catheter into Chloe's vein, she gave me an unrushed private moment with my girl. I told her how much I loved her and thanked her for helping me grow into a man. I thanked her for the well-being of my daughters and for all the service she selflessly gave. She told me with her eyes that she understood and that she was tired from fighting. She was ready to rest. As the life left her body, I cried harder than I ever had before or since. I loved my girl Chloe.

Chloe was quite a swimmer, and she had been delighted when we moved to our house on Lake Washington. A beaver lived under our dock and for years played a daily and spirited game of cat-and-mouse with poor Chloe. Chloe never caught that beaver. When Chloe started to slow down and could only sit on the step that led to the water, the beaver would come in close and sort of visit Chloe. After Chloe died, that poor beaver would search for Chloe every day, but finally gave up after a few weeks—missing her friend, I am quite sure.

When my girls got a bit older, they started to pine for a new dog. My traveling schedule dictated that we would need a dog that could travel with us. I had never had a small dog and never really even been around them. Yappy little dogs are not my style. We found our new little buddy—a Cavalier King Charles spaniel—after scouring dog breeds for months. What he lacks in smarts, he makes up for with love.

Our little boy, Buckley, asks for no more than some food and to be with us. He travels pretty much everywhere we go, and if I must travel on my own, he tries to sneak into my bag before I zip it up. He is always trying to go on man trips with me. I love you too, buddy.

Watching *Marley and Me* for the first time made me realize somehow that I have a full and rich life, that everyone has problems and fights and issues. But a strong family and an unruly dog are privileges and not nuisances.

Sure, I see myself as a sort of wandering bandolero at times, and I am allowed that in my family. They let me be who I am and I give back EVERYTHING I have in return.

I may mumble and grumble about living in a houseful of women at times, but really I don't know what I would do without them. I get to go out and rock like a badass (in my own mind, anyway) and ride my motorcycles like a hard-ass (again, that is how I view myself). Actually, I think I AM all of those things AND a damn good father and husband. Maybe lacking in romance at times and lacking in a general understanding of what little girls are all about. I am, however, the protector . . . and I know I have learned a lot of this from my life with dogs.

I miss my girls.

I'm ready to go home.

BE THE MAN

Set a good example. Even if you've got to fake it. Your kids observe everything you do. And even though it may not seem like it at the time, your kids want to be like you. They want to be proud of you and brag about their dad at school and to their friends. Be observant of your own actions around them kids.

Listen to your girl. We men sometimes get frustrated when our ladies talk. We will try to actually converse when she is deep into a story about the boss being a dick, or some other friend of hers doing your girl wrong. Do not even try to fix this situation! Your sweetie just wants you to listen. Hell, you don't even have to agree. Just listen. This is black-belt-level man stuff.

Do the dishes. Hell, take it one level further: cook the dinner and do the dishes. Doing laundry is man's work too, as well as cleaning up after the dogs and cuddling your kids. Having a home life where you get the opportunity to be a family man and partake in all these things is a very good thing. It means that you have elevated your man thing to the very top level. Keep it up.

Don't be a pussy. Don't shy away from a situation just because it's tough. If you need to protect the one you love or things are tough at work . . . pin those ears back and remember who the fuck you are.

Get smart. Educate yourself on what is going on in culture and politics. Read some books about history. Don't be a pawn, be a scholar.

Evolve. Our dads and granddads grew up in a different time. Communication and tenderness were not necessarily components of their age groups' makeup. You don't have to be exactly like them. Even though we saw good examples of man stuff in them, the times, they are a-changing.

FIND A GOOD WOMAN
(OR DUDE) AND HOLD HER CLOSE

BEFORE I LEARNED HOW TO COOK, THE ONLY JOB I could find as a teenager was digging ditches and working a jackhammer. It was grueling work. Don't get me wrong, I really like working hard. It's a trait that runs in my family. But I hate working through the flu.

One late-autumn, rainy-as-hell week in Seattle on my construction job, I was sick with the flu and couldn't afford to take any time off. So I went to work each day and dug the foundation for a three-car garage. By hand. Soaked to the bone with rain. I remember wanting nothing more than to get home to my bed. And that's exactly what I did at the end of each day of hell week.

When you're sick on tour, you don't get to go home at the end of the night. You have to wait for your gear to get loaded. You have to drive a few hundred miles. You have to sleep in a hotel room bed—if you get a bed at all. If you get to sleep at all.

As the Walking Papers' tour of Europe with Biffy Clyro was coming to an end, I could feel myself getting sicker and sicker. Digging ditches in the rain and cold didn't sound so bad: at least I could go home to my own bed every night. (I also made more money digging ditches than I did on the European tour, but that's beside the point . . .)

I practiced martial arts meditation about once an hour, trying to heal myself from within, keeping an eye out for the dark thoughts that can enter your mind when you're tired, hungry, sick, and lonely. I'm not the guy who tries to pull other people down with them. I wasn't broadcasting my misery. I was trying to be a productive member of the band. But my aches and fever were doing everything they could to keep me down. I had to continuously fight just to keep going.

When we made it to Brussels for the closing gig of the tour, I felt like I could see the finish line. I knew I'd be going home within the next twenty-four hours. I knew I'd be in my bed in thirty-six hours. I knew my wife and girls and farting dogs would be there waiting. Once my brain allowed those thoughts in, my body anticipated the relief that home would bring, and I had to fight extra hard.

I tried to hide it all from Susan. She thinks I work too hard as it is, and if she knew how sick I was on the road trying to break a new band, I knew it would give her fuel for a long talk about just what the hell I was doing. (I like to think that what decisions I make are always for the welfare of my family and rock and roll as a whole! And I hate trying to explain them!) Not only that, of course—I didn't want her to worry about me. Worrying doesn't do anyone any good.

All I really remember about the last show was saying good-bye to the guys in Biffy and their crew, and saying "great tour" to my Walking Papers brethren. I was too ill for an end-of-tour dinner after the gig and went straight to the airport hotel. Our tour manager, Jay, gave me a ride in the splitter. He helped check me in, looked at me like he was glad he didn't have what I had, and gave me a big hug good-bye. That was it. I had a 7 a.m. flight to Los Angeles via Chicago in the morning. As I got into bed, I hoped for the outside chance that I'd get better in the twenty-four hours it was going to take me to get home. It was December 15, and all I wanted was to be home with my family for Christmas—my favorite time of the year.

Then my phone rang: "Sir, it's 4:30 a.m. This is your wake-up call." Three hours of sleep hadn't made me feel any better. I woke up in a small pool of sweat. I knew that whatever I had wasn't catchable, as I'd been in close quarters with my band for the last two and a half weeks, and there wasn't even a collateral sniffle from any of them. I knew I wouldn't be spreading some deadly virus on the plane.

I slept off and on during the flight from Brussels to Chicago and was actually feeling somewhat OK walking through the giant terminals at O'Hare Airport. I gave Susan a call—from the States!—to check in. "We are so excited to see you," Susan said. "I'll be waiting in the cell lot when you get here!" *OK, babe. I'm almost home.* Surely I could just take some cold medicine and Advil on this last flight, and land in LA with a little pep in my step and color in my face. My plan was to fake it and quietly nurse myself back to full strength with the help of modern medicine.

My fever shot up on the flight to LA. No matter how much cold medicine I had in me, my bones and muscles continued to ache and throb. I slumped in my seat. I couldn't fight it anymore. Something was wrong with me beyond just a severe cold, flu, or sinus infection. Getting through that flight was an awful experience, and getting through the airport to baggage claim only escalated my fever and sickness. When Susan came around to pick me up, she took one look at me and said, "You are going to the doctor!"

In two days, we'd be flying to Seattle for Christmas, and I just wanted to be with my girls. I didn't *want* to go to the doctor's office. I didn't want to sit in a waiting room, and I didn't want to drive there. After chest x-rays, my doctor got a serious look on his face and told me that I'd had pneumonia for at least two weeks.

"We are *not* catching this early," he said. "This pneumonia has spread throughout your lungs. People *die* from this!" I've had this particular doctor for about ten years, and his bedside manner has not always been his strongest selling point. But I got his point. Rest. Antibiotics. More rest. X-rays every week. Stool sample (what does that have to do with your lungs?). Rest. Rest. Rest. More antibiotics, and then steroids. Exactly what I didn't want to do over Christmas break with my family.

But Susan and the girls looked after me, and I finally resigned myself to the fact that I wasn't going to be George Bailey for Christmas. I was simply just going to be a very sick Duff.

I've since learned not to push myself so hard. Supposedly, once a person has pneumonia, they are much more open to get it again. It's not something I ever want to face again, as this one occurrence of the illness took me nine weeks to finally rid my body of, and another eight to ten weeks to get my fitness back to where it was. This is not a way to end a great tour like we had.

The illness taught me to slow the fuck down, to keep an eye peeled for construction gigs—and it reminded me just what a wonderful woman I had to come home to.

After fifteen years of marriage—and even longer raising kids—we've both changed. It's normal. Keeping a relationship strong and exciting is an age-old dilemma. It starts with making the right decision about who you're going to spend the rest of your life with. Finding Susan is the best thing that's ever happened to me.

In finding the right person, you've got to have that initial gut feeling. Not the gut feeling you can convince yourself you had at some later point (we are all victims of this), but that very *first* feeling you have. If that initial feeling is "he/she is fucking weird/prick/ass/conceited," but you later convince yourself that he or she is "the one," you may very well be kicking yourself down the line for not following those initial feelings. I've fallen victim to this in the past. Hard.

My wife and I have survived eighteen years together because we *do* love each other. But that is not always enough. After the first two years of setting boundaries and expectations with your partner ("I WATCH FOOTBALL ON SUNDAYS!" or "YOU WILL GO TO THE FARMERS MARKET WITH ME ON SUNDAYS!") and after all of the control stuff settles down and you realize that you two aren't trying to change each other, then you will experience a calm. Don't let the calm trick you into thinking that there won't be any scrapes in your marriage. Fights will come, but it is so very important to figure out what the fight is really about, and not hold on to resentment. Sometimes fights simply occur because one of you is simply just tired or hungry. Just like resentments anywhere else in your life, holding on to them can destroy everything.

And there will be disagreements and differences of opinion.

For example, I like to think that I'm sooooo punk rock. I instinctively gravitate toward things that fit between the boundaries of what I think is punk-rock righteous. But when you're married and raising girls, those boundaries can get fuzzied in a hurry. Throw pillows are not punk rock. These little dog beds are not punk rock. This basket of shoes is not punk rock. This "Mi Casa es Tu Casa" sign is not punk rock.

That's OK. My wife and daughters do things differently than I do. In fact, I think the punk-rock ethic I come from cozies up quite nicely with being a husband, father, and dude who knows how to set a table.

My wife is a great woman. High morals, smart, and an incredible mother. She's also changed a lot since the day we met. She changes the things she's into about every two years. Men seem to hold on to their hobbies and habits longer and easier than women do, and keeping up with the churn of a lady's life can drive a guy crazy. I'm not trying to be sexist at all here, and, again, we have spent a lot of our time in Los Angeles, where all things are more transient. But this aforementioned dilemma seems to be a common experience with me and a ton of my dude friends. We just kind of watch and scratch our heads.

But as my wife's husband, I've had to go along on this ride with her, and I often am not in the loop to the "what's in, what's out" merry-go-round. I've stumbled into a few good walls with this lack of knowledge. "Hey, babe, let's go have dinner with so and so . . . " *BOINK*. No? Oh, she said something shitty on, uh, Instagram? Oh. Didn't you guys just go bike riding last weekend? Oh. OK. I see. *Right.* Because you went to dinner with so and so, she isn't talking to you? Right.

Punk-rock dudes like me and my dude friends just don't go through this kind of stuff. It's actually pretty much totally incomprehensible. But I have to have her back in all of this and hug her when she gets hurt by this kind of stuff. It hurts her. I can't chuckle like I used to (thinking it was all sort of silly). Hurt is *real*, and that is what I, as her husband, have to understand.

I know my wife has my back through everything, and she knows that I have hers. This simple understanding is stronger than anything else in a marriage. Your mate *has* to believe in you. Period. My career and life have had a few exceptional ups and downs (like everyone's), and so has my wife's. It's the belief in each other, unquestioning and without judgment, that sends a good marriage into the upper echelons of a *great* marriage.

Keeping things nasty and kick-ass in the boudoir is key, too. Keep that shit high and tight, gentlemen. Make time and plan special events so that the two of you can have some alone time. Hell, I love the idea of making appointments. It's kinda dirty. Done right, it gives you both something to look forward to. Being together for some good sexy time has a way of alleviating all kinds of crap that can muddy a marriage.

Breathe. Take a walk. Spend time apart. Try to make those times that you are together special and full of life. Your marriage should be the break from the noise of your work life. Above all, keep working on your marriage. There's always work to be done.

A few weeks before our fifteenth wedding anniversary, the girls went away for six days, and the fray and fun chaos that is our family life suddenly came to an abrupt stop. It was just Susan and me alone in the house.

After seventeen years of sheer madness, the sudden recognition that this was the way it was gonna be in no time at all hit us hard. The girls are going to be off to college before we blink. What do we have in common now without the kids? The both of us had changed to a certain degree since we were last alone together some eighteen years prior. What now? What are WE going to do?

This is what was on our minds when we flew to Hawaii to celebrate our anniversary. We were both mentally overreacting to what kind of life the *two* of us were going to have once the girls were gone.

It turned out to be the perfect time to start figuring it out. Our anniversary trip was magical. And although neither of us verbalized it, we both were relieved to discover that, yes, we are still into each other *very* much. We had a ton of fun, just the two of us, and started talking about future adventures we could set out upon.

I made the case for climbing in the Himalayas and seeing the Buzzcocks *in* Manchester. She has her heart set on leisurely strolls in tropical climates and seeing a reunited Duran Duran.

We'll sort it out.

PARENT. EVEN IF IT'S VIA SKYPE

It's a family tradition to get our Christmas tree together from our favorite lot in Seattle. I was sick, my girls knew it, and it took a bit of the fun out of the anticipation of the moment. But I love Christmas. And I was determined to soldier on. I got out of bed, took some cold medicine, popped some Advil, wrapped myself up in a bunch of warm clothes, and threw on my raincoat. We weren't coming back without a tree. When we got to the lot, it was so blustery and cold that my girls knew I shouldn't venture out into the elements. I decided to stay in the car, and Mae went and picked out our tree. "Dad," she said, "you just stay warm, and I'll find the right one."

It was the first time that the role of caretaker had reversed. This show of concern from my daughter took my breath away. It told me that she loved me and wanted me to get better. It showed me that I was right to have that hurt when I was away, and that our parenting helped make Mae the young woman she has become. I felt comforted and feel comfort now as I write this. I can go out again on the road and feel that pain again, the pain that reminds me of how lucky I am to have what I have.

As a dad who works on the road, I know that I have missed a ton of cool and important things in my kids' childhood. That's why I cling to moments such as this. It is a tough deal to be a touring musician and love your kids as much as I do. Saying all of that, I hope I never find a way to turn off the hurt when I am gone. That hurt is a by-product of the love I have for my family. Coming home is always exciting, even when the teenagers barely say "s'up" and go straight to their rooms and shut the doors.

When it comes to teenagers, a parent's role is more like that of a guidance counselor. I once saw Collin Cowherd put it well on ESPN's *The Herd* one morning, talking about a conversation he had with his fourteen-year-old daughter regarding the poor behavior of some pro athlete. He made the comment that he tutors her to make good decisions, but that he is more of a consultant to her at this point than a parent. He was right on.

We parented a ton to these kids when they were smaller and around us all of the time. But now that they are with their friends and schoolmates, your job has largely been done. Now you hope they will make good decisions about whose car they get into after school or how they behave in public and on social media. You hope they make the right decisions based on examples laid down by us parents. Susan and I will guide them from the sidelines here at home, but we don't get to play in the games so much anymore. We're more like consultants. And ringmasters. Times like that day at the Christmas tree lot, it feels good to see that we've done a little bit of something right.

I learned a lot about parenting from watching my parents—both good and bad.

I had a great childhood because I had a great mom. Sure, things weren't always rosy between her and me (as no parent/child relationship is without some testing by the child), and I was a complete ass to her in my early teens. But her steely reserve, smarts, and kind nature always made me think twice before I pulled an asshole move. She was fantastic.

There were eight of us kids, and by the time I came around (as the last born), my mom had her wisdom on *point*. She never made snap judgments or tried to prove a point by yelling. If I got frustrated trying to do something, she'd instruct me to "just breathe and relax" before I tried again whatever it was that was giving me trouble. She had an arsenal of powerful little idioms for every occasion that she exuded in spades. I've drawn on them in times of need for my entire life, long past the end of hers.

After Susan and I brought Grace home from the hospital, I started to wonder exactly how I was going to be able to care for our baby. I hadn't had any real sleep in more than a week and was beyond frustrated. I called my mom for some advice. "Mom, just how in the hell did you do this? You had EIGHT kids, and I don't even know how to deal with one!" Her voice was calm and Zen in her reply: "Just breathe, honey. You will get this thing. Those babies survive anything, and you will sleep sometime soon."

The bad stuff I learned from my folks stemmed from the things you know are crappy deals when you witness them as a kid as well as incidents that reveal themselves as wrong when you become an adult. I saw infidelity when I was seven years old and knew it wasn't cool. I also got to witness the fallout of those infidelities and the hurt they caused. Those eyewitness experiences colored my life in a positive way. As a young boy, I decided that I wouldn't let infidelity be a part of my life when I started a family. It still isn't.

My parents divorced when I was in second grade. Because I hadn't developed any real coping abilities, I didn't speak to my father for five years. As I grew older, I was able to come to grips with their divorce, and my father once again became a part of my life. But I grew up mostly under the tutorship of my mom and older siblings.

I loved both my parents and appreciated everything they did for me. Like me, as young parents, they didn't know what they were doing—how could anyone until they're doing it for themselves? We hold our parents to such lofty ideals, and in the end they are just people faced with the fact that they are suddenly raising kids. When I became a parent myself, I let go of any and all residual blame.

I've taken what I learned from my mom, and also what I discovered about my dad, and morphed all of those experiences into a parenting style of my own. I've learned that there are no "normal" circumstances in which to parent, but the important thing is to parent. Period. Whether you're a single parent, a busy parent, or a dad who provides for his family by traveling the globe.

The father of girls will do absolutely *anything* for the welfare or benefit of his daughters. There is a lesson in that. If you give your daughter too much and make things too easy, she will not grow. This is an early struggle that has yet to subside for this father. You cannot kick the ass of everyone your daughter has a struggle with (even though that is your first instinct). You cannot buy her ice cream every time she wants it (even though being at the ice cream shop with your daughter is one of the happiest moments in life for the both of you). You *cannot* talk about periods or feminine hygiene products or anything that even comes close to this (even though you are just trying to understand why your daughter is suddenly IRATE at you).

Girls are so much different from boys. Watching your own girls grow up and go through all their unique stages gives us fathers a much bigger insight into the female gender. Hell, it's given me the knowledge and insight to understand my wife and sisters and female friends better. It takes patience. We men are just built differently. I'm sure if a mother of boys is reading this right now, she'd say the same thing from the opposite viewpoint. A guy like me has to sit patiently and observe before I act, and guys just really aren't born with patience and observational skills. At least I wasn't.

When my girls were born, I was able to clear away the busyness in my life and attain a strong bond with both of them. We did everything together. And, like all parents do with their kids, we invented our own little games. One of our favorites was tickle time. I'd be the Green Hornet, and Mae was Kato. She'd pounce on me at any time—usually unannounced. We'd wrestle and tumble, and she'd always win. This was always our time, and we'd belly laugh and have some of the most fun of our lives.

It used to be that the girls couldn't wait to hang out with me and cuddle up next to me to watch TV. But something happens between a father and daughter when she gets close to eleven years of age. That something is that they suddenly realize that *you are a boy!* Gross. And just like that, the cuddling and tickle times and bedtime stories are out the window. It's a very hard time for us dads. Kinda brutal, actually. It sucks to suddenly get cast into the category of *yuck* right along with all of the snot-faced eleven-year-olds.

When Grace was this age, Susan and I thought we had done something wrong. We had no experience with the pre-teen change. Our baby became a totally different person. She didn't want to walk *with* us to school anymore, when this used to be such a special time for our family. *Oh, my gosh, Mom and Dad, you have to be kidding me! There is no way I am going to hold your hand walking across the street! SO embarrassing!!!* She wouldn't talk to us and would go straight to her room after school. We thought something was seriously wrong and were about to call for some kind of outside professional help, when another mom said to us: "Oh, right. Grace is about to get her first period." This mother of an older girl wised us up real quick. "It'll be a couple years until she comes back to you guys. Especially *you,* Dad. But she *will* come back." A couple of years?

A good friend of mine had gone through all of these changes with his oldest daughter some years before we did. His daughter was in her late teens when we went through it, and I found myself calling him and his wife often to get insight on just who my daughters *were.* Really. It is so totally gnarly for a father to suddenly "lose" his little girls, who transform into Tasmanian Devil–like blurs of emotion and anger in the shape of what was once your tickle partner.

I started to tour again just after I got out of Seattle U. Grace and Mae were seven and four years old the first time I brought them on tour with Velvet Revolver. Along with singer Scott Weiland and our wives, we decided to get a shared family tour bus in Europe, and away we went. I knew the girls had never seen me on a stage, and I was curious about how this experience would play out in their kid minds. After watching a couple shows from the side of the stage, Grace came up to me on the bus one night and said, "Dad, you guys swear too much onstage." Hmmm. She was right. One of the many upsides of taking the kids on the road is that they keep you in check.

When the girls got older and it was harder to get them out of school, we turned to Skype. Among other things, Skype made it easy for me to help the girls with their homework. I had just retaken all of my math in college, and that became my go-to subject to help the girls with. They used to get super psyched when they saw my face on the computer and would always answer my Skype request for a video chat. But for teenagers, I've learned that it's a bit nerdy to Skype with your parents. It's made parenting from afar a bit trickier— but no less manageable.

First off: You must have a *great* partner, and, in my case, I have a great wife. The most important decision any man or woman will *ever* make is picking the person they will spend their life with. I made a couple not-thought-out decisions on marriage in my old drinking days, but I instinctively knew I shouldn't have kids yet. It wasn't until I was sober and met Susan that I was sure I wanted to have kids. I knew she and I would be together to raise them. This, I am quite sure, has made a huge difference on being a parent for me, and for my daughters. Again, *who* you have kids with will always be the very most important decision you ever make. They should really teach that stuff at school.

Susan does everything she can to minimize the separation pains when I am gone. For instance, the girls may not want to Skype anymore, but when Susan picks one of our daughters up from school, they will both call me on the car speaker-phone. Susan figured out that by having them *both* call it forces the too-cool teenager to actually speak on the phone.

But I still miss Skyping with my girls. When those old habits go away, parents feel that separation. Your kids want to be independent, and you just want your kids back. It's a slippery slope that we parents have to adjust to. In a lot of ways, it is another step deeper into becoming a full-fledged grown-up. My wife and I have had to grow up a lot over the last few years and adapt to the changing role we play in our daughters' lives. (BTW, who says that us parents really are grown-ups anyway? In a lot of ways, I still want to be a kid and have tantrums and have shit go *my* way all of the time.)

Just as I was at my wit's end when *both* girls were fully into this preteen and teenage miasma and angst, things started to change.

With Grace, it happened almost overnight. She literally came out of her bedroom one day with three songs she had written. She had been so removed from me that I had no idea she was even into writing or performing music. I'd assumed she was in her room writing manifestos on how to get away with the perfect plot to alienate her parents forever. She came out of her room one day and said, "Hey, Dad! Can I play you some music?" And just like that, I was back in the game.

In her time away, Grace had morphed into a thoughtful and interesting young person. As parents, we understood that our kids would be watching our every action, even in those times when we assumed they were putting every last inch of effort into ignoring us. Susan and I had just kept on as we went through these periods with the girls, even though this tension would do its darnedest to pit us against each other at times. We'd treat each other with love and respect, and Grace suddenly came out of her room that day, with those same qualities. It was really quite stunning.

Mae was still quite "away" at this point (Grace was *late* fifteen, and Mae had just turned thirteen). But now Grace and I had a common thing in this newfound interest she gained in music. In her time away, Grace had stopped listening to Bieber, Swift, and Katy Perry and supplanted it all with Bowie, Iggy, Lou Reed, Grimes, and the Yeah Yeah Yeahs. For the most part, she was listening to the *exact* music that I listened to at that age, and I could now hang in her room again and talk music and pick out songs on her growing, cool-as-fuck iTunes library. We even started going to the record store together.

Ben and Jeff from Walking Papers agreed to record Grace's music in Jeff's basement studio. Jeff, having two girls just two years respectively younger than mine, marveled at the new Grace. Seeing Grace come out of her teenage hideout gave Jeff sparkling hope for his future relationship with his own daughters. The songs she wrote were really good, and the finished product from Jeff's basement pushed Grace to the next step of wanting to start a band. *This,* of course, was okay with me.

At the time, I was getting ready to present a keynote address in New York at the burgeoning CBGBs Music and Film Festival. The brand CBGBs alone garners a ton of respect and attention, and one day leading up to my departure, I received an e-mail from the owner of the festival stating that he'd heard that my daughter had a band, and . . . would they like to play the festival? They thought it'd be cool to introduce a new generation of talent, and her being my daughter (and I had actually played CBGBs) added a cool back story. Great for press and all.

The conversation with Grace went something like this:

Me: "Hey, Grace! You want to play your first gig in New York for the CBGBs Festival? You know, CBGBs, where Blondie and Iggy and The Ramones played?"

Grace: "WHAAAAAAAAAAAAAAAAAT!!!! OHHHHH MMMMMMYYYYYYY GAAAAAAAAWD!"

That was a yes.

Mae started to pay attention to the changes her sister was going through. Susan and I tried not to give too much weight to what Grace was doing. We didn't want the extra attention on her older sibling to push Mae further into her teenage hole. But Grace was engaging us all the time now, and it was tough to hide our excitement and happiness. Then, sort of naturally and out of the blue, Mae started suggesting that she do her sister's makeup for an upcoming photo shoot before we left for NYC. It turns out that Mae had been in her room for the last two years studying hundreds of different YouTube makeup teachers. Homegirl now suddenly had some serious *skills!*

Music? I can help out with and be something of a mentor. Makeup? Uh, not so much. But this is where we dads improvise and do our damnedest to take part in whatever it is our kids do. Susan was much more key to drawing Mae out of her hole with this new interest in makeup, but I tried. For Christmas, I went to a beauty supply store by myself and asked the people there if they could help me find some sort of makeup kit for my thirteen-year-old who was totally into this stuff. I was so excited when I wrapped up her presents. Of course, I had no idea what it all was. But, *still*, this was going to be a total home run for old Pops.

On Christmas morning, I could barely contain my excitement for her to open her gifts. She seemed totally psyched about the stuff I got her, and she actually gave me a hug. I knew later that this was a big step in her growing out of her teenager-ness. The items that I got her were apparently all wrong. But she didn't act disappointed in that moment and, rather, gave her dad a hug for just the thought of me trying. The thought of that kind of stuff from my girls buckles my knees.

The day after Christmas, Mae asked if we could have tickle time—for the first time in almost three long years.

A few days later, I experienced one of the best nights of my life. Grace's band, the Pink Slips, was asked to open for my band on New Year's Eve in Seattle. Here I was at home, where I started my whole music experience, and my daughter's band—now including Alice in Chains' drummer Sean Kinney's nephew, Keenan, on drums—was starting its career. A lot of our family came, as did my old pal Sean and a bunch of his family. It was New Year's Eve, and I was with people I loved.

Not long after, Mae (now fourteen years old and 5'9"!) came into the kitchen. I was there, busy doing something or other and caught her out of the corner of my eye. I kind of freaked out, because literally I thought it was Susan, and so I said "Hi, Babe!" my usual greeting to my wife. "Hi, *Dad!*" My wife is a statuesque beauty, with an easy smile and built-in charm. Now my little girl, our baby and "little peach," is also a statuesque beauty. Oh, boy. Hey, at least I got tickle time back in the fold! I'll worry about boys soon enough. Until then, I'll just enjoy having Mae back from her teenage hideout.

Grace had her senior homecoming this year. Boys and dating have taken a backseat to her music, and so we haven't really had to deal with boy drama since she was about fifteen. Grace wanted to go to her homecoming this year, realizing she should at least try to experience some of these early life milestones. Her guitar player, Charlie, is a senior at the same school, and they agreed to go together as a date. He is a really great dude, and they are easy friends and grown-up enough to think this would be a fun move for the both of them. Grace was playing it cool, sort of acting like this whole thing was no big deal.

I've noticed that girls at her high school dress a bit too Kardashian-like at these types of events: showing too much skin and wearing heels that are way too high. A few days before homecoming, I noticed that she was putting together an outfit and that she had scheduled a hair appointment. On homecoming night, her friends met at our house for pictures. Charlie showed up looking cool as hell in a smart, European-cut black suit. A few minutes later, Grace came out of her room. Her light blue dress was so classy, showing only arms. She chose very small and gorgeous heels, and her blue eyes shone as bright as her smile. She is a *young woman* now, and Charlie and I kind of gasped at the same time. Stunning. My girls are not girls anymore.

But they will *always* be my little girls, until the end.

⌣

Two months after Christmas, I was back in Europe with the Walking Papers, opening for Aerosmith for three weeks. It was a great opportunity for us. But it presented something of a quandary for my family. When I started to tour again post-GN'R, my girls were in preschool and elementary school, and I promised that I wouldn't be away from them for more than two weeks. I wanted them to always know I was coming back and to know I miss them. I try to make it seem like I'm not gone at all. Flying back across the country for a single day off is not uncommon, and I get all the school e-mails and am in direct contact with the teachers and other parents.

I didn't want to break our two-week rule, so I used airline miles to fly Susan and the girls out to meet me for the last week. The girls would be out of school, and Susan could even come out a couple days prior so that she and I could have a little fancy time.

The girls were well equipped to fly by themselves to London from Seattle. They have flown more than most adults and know the ins and outs of international air travel and customs. But, of course, and to their great dismay, we got them an unaccompanied minor escort (offered by all airlines). When we picked them up at Heathrow, Grace was totally embarrassed that she had to have a flight attendant with them all the way through customs, baggage claim, and finally to meet us. "She called me 'Sweetie,' Dad. *Sweetie!* I'm *sixteen,* you know!"

I've missed you, too, honey.

But on the drive into London, Grace got very excited about a local discovery. Blondie was going to be playing in town the next night, and she wanted the two of us to go. Blondie has been one of my favorites since I was Grace's age.

Yes, babe. We can indeed go see Blondie.

It's always comforting to see my girls make the right choices. It makes me feel like our parenting has rocked pretty well so far.

It's been such an absolute blessing and honor to be the father of two girls. There was no way I could've imagined at, say, the age of twenty that this would eventually be my fate. There would have been no way to prepare myself for this, even if I *had* somehow known beforehand (I think most guys somehow just assume that when they have a kid, it will be a boy. I've talked about this topic with a lot of my friends over the years, and it's nearly unanimous. Weird, right?).

Being the father of girls *only* instantly enlists you in a unique club. We fellow travelers give each other *deep*-respect nods when we bump into each other along the path of life. We know that we have been put here to be a man-guide for these special ladies, and it is the best thing ever, because of how much we get to learn about ourselves as men through our girls.

DATE LIKE YOU MEAN IT

WHEN MY GIRLS STARTED FETCHING THE ATTENTION of the opposite sex, I had to lay down a few ground rules, as all parents do. Things must stay classy.

But it's not just teenagers and singles who should keep the dating aboveboard. Adults—and especially married men like me . . . especially me—need to be reminded of the basics every once in a while.

Be a rocker. This occupation helped me get through the awkward "dating years," as I really never dated at all until I got sober. Those early years were basically filled with postgig hookups or some other male-female interaction as a result of dark, loud, booze-filled haunts. Of course, I was pretty much hammered all the time until I was thirty and experienced TWO bad (but thankfully short) marriages. You don't have to be a musician to be a rocker: to rock is to have self-confidence, to be comfortable in your own skin, something I didn't truly achieve until years after I became sober. Which reminds me . . .

Get sober. Damn, what a scary prospect my first sober date was. I really didn't know how to act. What was I supposed to talk about? What if I got food on my face? I know I wouldn't even have cared before. So many things were going through my head that I probably came off as some sort of weird loser with no social skills. Those first dates after I got sober were some of the most horrible, failure-filled times in my life. "Hooking up" was definitely the last thing on my mind. But of course, in the end, sobriety and the choices that I make when sober are really and truly mine.

Open the door for your date. Especially if it's to your bedroom. Old-fashioned values and courteousness never go out of style. Pulling the chair out at the restaurant is also a classy move. Opening car doors and shedding your jacket for a woman when it is nippy are two things that should become habit for you guys out there. Your date will appreciate these gentlemanly gestures, and she will never tire of them.

Mind the three As: attention, affection, and appreciation. These are three things that women crave and that we men don't easily or naturally dole out. The three As are applicable in matters big and small, and they shouldn't be tossed off as unimportant kowtowing to your chick. She will respond in a positive manner, and that is good for you both. It helps if you actually mean the things you say, but it's not always necessary. Here are two examples, one bad and one good. Bad: "Hey, you, you are HOT! [Attention.] Give me a hug! [Affection.] That felt good! [Appreciation.]" Good: "Are you wearing new lip gloss? Let me kiss you! I like it!" Actually, both of these would work, and neither of them are stellar, but you get the idea.

Bonus tip for the ladies: make your man feel important. Men are pretty simple. We require very little, in fact, to make us happy. I think we feel more vital and "hot" when we are successful in our chosen field. This probably comes from our instincts as the hunter and provider. When you "bring food back to the cave," you are appreciated and important. I think relationships fail more often when this mutual appreciation breaks down or is ignored.

Wear something sexy underneath. My Seattle Seahawks (Sea Gals) cheerleader lingerie had usually been my "go-to" undergarment to make myself feel good and surprise a lucky girl if the night went that far! You get the drift.

Don't text your date. I believe that protocol during the embryonic period of dating should be as text-free as possible. This early time in a relationship should be nothing short of poetic, and it actually used to be called courting. Phone calls and sweet notes are far and away the best way to a woman's or man's heart. An unexpected delivery of flowers or chocolates shows women your sensitive side; even Cary Grant would be proud. Don't tell all your "boys" every last detail, thus spoiling an intimate place reserved in your heart. The same goes for us married fellas, too. Just because we've been with the same woman for a few years doesn't mean she's lost her taste for romance. A nice note goes a long way.

Never split the bill on a first date. I'm old school; the man should pick up the tab. I do realize this is perhaps an antiquated way of thinking, but you can suck it!

NEVER say someone else's name in the throes of lovemaking. Again, I'm old school! If you mistakenly call out your old girlfriend's name, make some shit up, and QUICK! This is the one instance when I can condone lying. If you can't remember the name of the person you're with, may I suggest coming up with some kick-ass moniker that you can remember. You will have to call that person by the same name tomorrow, after all! While a name like "my little Irish whorelette" may be good after a couple of cocktails and thence into the "sack," it probably won't work well in the morning with coffee and a danish.

Protect your daughters. Fellas, we all know what boys want. And all of you fathers of daughters know the horror of that first boy coming by to pick up your little girl. Short of brandishing a shotgun when you open the front door, I've discovered a different weapon: your cell phone. Let me explain:

When the first dude shows up at the door, take the young buck to the side and explain the ground rules: "Hey, bud. My name is Duff and I am Grace's daddy. Now, I want you guys to have a really excellent time tonight. As a matter of fact, let me store my phone number in your cell. Now, listen, I would like it if you had her back home by eleven. Oh, and just remember this: EVERYTHING THAT YOU DO OR TRY WITH MY DAUGHTER TONIGHT, I WILL DO TO YOU WHEN YOU GET BACK TO MY HOME. Great, now that that is FULLY understood, have a wonderful time and call me if you need anything at all."

KEEP YOUR FRIENDS CLOSE

AS PARADIGM CHANGING AS IT WAS FOR MY DAUGHTER to not only express interest in the same things as me, but to solicit and appreciate my help, something else monumental was percolating that seemed no less consequential: my Seahawks were winning. All the time.

The Walking Papers guys, and really, a majority of musicians that I know, aren't big sports fans. In high school, there is the classic jock/artsy crowd split. A lot of young musicians simply veer away from sports at that age because of the youthful sneering from the "jock crowd."

To hell with the jock/rock divide. I've been a Hawks fan as long as I can remember.

In 2006, my friend Alice in Chains guitarist Jerry Cantrell joined Susan and me at Super Bowl XL to watch the Hawks play the Steelers in Detroit. When we got married, Susan understood that being a Seahawks fan was part of the deal if we were going to have a loving, long-term relationship. The geeked-out excitement I had for that game was quickly extinguished by a lop-sided flag-throwing contest where all the calls went against my beloved team. Before the game, it seemed so obvious that our team would not make a great national story as winners of the Super Bowl. Seattle wouldn't draw a huge TV audience and sell tons of TV ads. Am I saying the outcome was predestined? Well, I'm not saying that it wasn't. We got burned. We went back to our little corner of the United States, licked our wounds, and home grew the 12th Man.

Here we were, entering the playoffs, ready for another shot.

As sick as I was, I rallied and made it to the Hawks' final regular season game, a few days before New Year's Eve. But my doctor made it clear to me that the first playoff game was out of the question. All I could do was lie in bed and take antibiotics. With a victory against the Saints out of the way, we were one win away from returning to the Super Bowl. And who would we be playing? Our archrivals: the 49ers.

This I couldn't miss. I'd been with my team all season, and I couldn't let them down now.

⌣

The season began just as Walking Papers took its place on the Uproar Tour, a traveling festival that invited us to headline its second stage right as our first record was coming out in America. It was an excellent opportunity for the band to get that vaunted US mainstream hard rock exposure, and we jumped at the chance. As much as I was looking forward to the opportunity, I was a bit apprehensive, since we'd be touring during the start of football season.

When you're in a touring band, where and how you will be spending your football Sundays becomes a part-time job. And guys like me, with a wife and kids in school, also have to figure out how and when to get back home during a tour as lengthy as this, not to mention when and where I can do my daily fitness stuff. I was about to turn fifty, and I wanted to be able to kick life's ass like a he-man at this pivotal juncture in my life.

Lucky for me, Alice in Chains were on the Uproar Tour, too. My longtime Hawks superfan pal, Jerry, offered to get the DirecTV Sunday NFL football package on his bus. There it was. The problem of finding a sports bar or Applebee's was averted. We'd be able to watch at least the first four weeks of the season on Jerry's bus.

Jerry and I have been friends since the late '80s. We've both had some serious ups and downs in our lives, and our friendship has deepened as we've seen our respective bands go through hell, or, far worse, witnessed friends and bandmates perish. A large component of what bonds us is our mutual love of the Hawks. I'm not trying to sound funny here, but our football team became a constant in some of our most chaotic and dark times. Sports can be a powerful thing.

We had just lost our beloved Seattle Supersonics; our Mariners hadn't had anything on the field to compete on a high level since 2001. All we really had was our Seahawks.

The tour moved from the Gorge Amphitheater in central Washington to Portland, Oregon, the evening before the first football Sunday of 2013. Since Jerry had already invited me to his bus to watch all the games, he furthered the invitation by seeing if I wanted to crash on one of his spare bunks. Jerry splurged on himself for the tour by scoring a bus of his own to help accommodate what's important. JC supplanted some real shitty and unhealthy things in his life with some new white stuff: golf balls!

I love the guys in the Walking Papers, and I think they feel the same about me, but a day away can do wonders for everyone involved (although I have no idea just how they got along without me).

The Walking Papers bus had the twelve-bunk configuration (six per side). Jerry's bus had two per side. Since there were only four bunks on Jerry's bus, they were absolutely huge. He even sent someone to get me coffee, a must if you know me. All of this is pure luxury at this point on the tour. I slept like a damn rock.

Jane's Addiction were also on this tour. Little did Jerry and I know, but JA singer extraordinaire Perry Farrell is, like us, a total NFL geek. His wife, Etty, texted me Saturday night and asked if Perry could come watch with us. He didn't want to invite himself, and his wife sort of set up an adult playdate.

If you've ever seen Perry perform, then you know he is edgy and flamboyant and, I think, the second coming of Iggy. But a football fan? I was surprised. It's not like Perry is a stranger to me. We've been on the road together. And for a brief time I sat in with his band.

I woke up at 8:30 on Sunday morning. I could hear the NFL Network pregame show cranking from the front lounge and could smell the coffee brewing as I stumbled out of my bunk. My football-watching pal was already fully engaged in what would be the first of a sixteen-game ritual. He had fantasy football up on his computer, snacks were open, and his Hawks hat was firmly ensconced on his dome.

The New York Jets were playing the early game. Since we were on the West Coast, it started at 10 a.m. The Jets have been Perry's team since he was a kid and Joe Namath was their quarterback. If Perry was gonna come over to our bus, it'd be for this game for sure.

Now, here is the deal when you have the DirecTV football package at home or on your bus: whoever is the owner of said package also gets to control which games are being watched and switched between. It just isn't proper football code to insist on watching your game when you're the guest. But Jerry conceded that if Perry came over, he'd be happy to have the Jets game on somewhat when the Hawks weren't playing.

Before we move on here, I'd like to point out how much I admire people like Perry Farrell. Perry don't give a fuck about what anyone thinks of him. He is a true free spirit, with a heart consisting of parts lion, child, killer, and saint.

He is a true weirdo, in the best sense of that word. I've seen him at home, as the gentle baseball-coach dad to his son's teams. I've seen his eyes onstage, when shit gets very real, and he is a man possessed (and something I wish we had way more of in rock and roll). I've even witnessed him get all "street" on some dude who was trying to be all tough and threatening on some shitty street corner in Hollywood.

But I'd never watched a football game with Perry. There are certain unspoken rules in place while watching that go beyond insisting on your game: You don't talk about antiquing or clothes shopping. You don't talk about how some new hand-hewn wood flooring would "look great in your entryway." You don't talk about people in your band or your wife or girlfriend or boyfriend. It's football Sunday! When we do speak, it's about fucking football. Got it?

Perry showed up at the bus with a bottle of red wine. Red flag. He didn't want to come empty-handed, and since he was sharing his bus with Etty and the female dancers for Jane's Addiction, it's all he could muster. It alarms guys like Jerry and me when a fella brings a bottle of red wine to the game for the above-mentioned reasons. Red wine bringing is dangerously close to clothes shopping.

Our fears, however, were instantly allayed when Perry followed his entrance with a vocal and informed tirade about the new possession-out-of-bounds rule that the NFL was trying out. Neither Jerry nor I even knew about it, so we fake nodded like we were just as miffed as Perry about the situation. Perry went on to school us on the holes that the

Jets needed to fill—team, coaching staff, and personnel—if they stood a chance of getting to the playoffs.

Perry could be a goddamn NFL commentator. I'd almost forgotten: the dude is good at everything.

Perry drank that bottle of red, and Jerry and I watched him get more animated and thrust himself into the game. Unfortunately, his team lost.

When it came time for the Seahawks, Perry, sensing the blue and teal blood pulsating through our veins, started to wax poetic and informatively about how the Seahawks made sense this year, how good he thought the "system" of Coach Pete was and how good Coach Pete and GM Schneider were at finding gems in the lower draft brackets. How the hell did this guy know so much about our team?

We realized then and there that Perry is an NFL historian and aficionado. Don't judge a book by its cover, people.

He will always be welcome to our future football-watching sessions. I may have to call him next year for advice on my fantasy football picks.

As for Jerry and me, we watched our Hawks beat the Carolina Panthers and knew that we were in for a special season.

⌣

Before the playoff game against the 49ers—the game that would decide which team would compete in Super Bowl XLVIII—the city of Seattle started to go ballistic and I started to feel a little better. Slowly. I went to my doctor again and asked if there weren't something he could do so that I could go to the game. I could see in his eyes that he understood me. He understood that I had waited since I was twelve years old for a team and a season like this. He switched me up to the heaviest dose of antibiotic offered, told me to dress warm and stay dry, and wished my team the best of luck.

Feeling better started to put my brain back in the right place again, too. The old "healthy body, healthy mind" adage is really quite true. I started to fantasize about how far my team could go, and though I'd never audibly say the words "Super Bowl" for fear of jinxing my boys, I did realize that the Super Bowl would land two days before my fiftieth birthday. What if? I mean . . . just imagine?! Turning fifty, for me, began to have the old pre-illness appeal again.

With doctor's approval and Jerry at my side, we made our way to Century Link Field in Seattle for what was one of the most consequential sports moments in our city's history. Century Link sits on hallowed ground. Before it was Century Link, the property was home to a large, important multiuse facility called the Kingdome. It was a homely venue, sure, but I'd be lying if I said I didn't get a bit emotional when it imploded (literally). It played host to the Hawks, the Mariners, and even some Sonics games. It's also where some of the most consequential musical moments of my life took place.

I played there with Guns N' Roses in 1992, and my whole family was able to come out and see what we were up to—for better and for worse. But that night at the Dome wasn't nearly as important to me as the night I spent there fifteen years prior.

I saw Led Zeppelin at the Kingdome on July 17, 1977, when I was thirteen years old. It was the event in my life that seemingly nothing else would or could ever compare to. I mean, how could anything ever come close to seeing Led Zeppelin live, in their prime as a thirteen-year-old boy? Way back then, my three best friends (present tense still applies—we are still best friends) and I all stood in line at the record store at 10 a.m. on a Saturday morning to buy ten-dollar general admission tickets to see Led Zeppelin.

We got our tickets at Cellophane Square, a record shop in Seattle's University District that had just started to become a central gathering point for my group of friends. Before the Internet, *the* place to find out about new and essential music was at the record store. Cellophane Square had a little pinball room in the back, as well, so little shits like us would end up hanging out at the place—listening to music and playing pinball for hours after school and on weekends. Heading down there to wait in line for Led Zeppelin tickets just added another layer of coolness to our favorite record store. Shit! I got turned on to the Sex Pistols, learned pinball cool, *and* got Led Zeppelin tickets at Cellophane Square. For a thirteen-year-old, it was the coolest place on earth.

The thing about holding general admission tickets is that you don't have a reserved place. The first ones to the venue are the first ones through the door. First ones through the door get the best place on the floor, closest to the band. In the '70s, it was common to go down to the venue the day or night before the concert to camp out in line to be in the first-wave, best-seat/standing-place category. The practice is now illegal because of trampling deaths, but it was just the way it was done back then. Even as thirteen-year-old kids, we knew we'd have to somehow get down to the Kingdome way early the morning of the show to have a chance at getting anywhere close to Zeppelin. Our Gods. The Chosen Four. The best there ever was.

The four of us little dudes were already trying to form a band, and the term "punk rock" was being whispered from somewhere deep and dark in downtown Seattle. But for now, we'd have to wait in line with the Columbian shake pot we brought and the bologna and Velveeta sandwiches our moms forced on us as we scrambled to catch the #75 bus downtown.

We waited in that line all day. We saw older girls—maybe sixteen, seventeen—who we thought were real women! They had jean shorts on, lipstick, feathered hair, and . . . uh . . . boobs! This was badass. No one looked at us like we were kids, and no one grumbled at the surely low quality of our non-bud bud. And hell, the hours and minutes were getting smaller to see sonofabitchin' LED ZEPPELIN!

(As a side note: My own daughters are now the age of those girls I just mused about in that last little bit. It's a little weird to ponder back to that age while also being a father. Just a thought. Don't get all freaked out about it, alright?)

As it got closer and closer to showtime, we noticed that the crowd outside the Dome had grown large. Close to 20,000 fans were waiting to get in. They started to chant: "We want in! We want in!"

When we finally got in, we found a great place to see the show. There was no opener. Just Zeppelin. From the opening moments of "The Song Remains the Same" through the epic finale of "Rock and Roll," we knew every riff, drum beat, guitar solo, and lyric. This was our first real rock concert, and the air was thick with pot smoke and the overwhelming scent of Teen Spirit. Seattle didn't get all of the big tours back then, so when big bands did come through, I think they most definitely were overcome with the absolute riotous din that came from our rock-starved region. Seattle always has been a little louder.

The band played harder for us that night. We knew they were putting everything into it for us. The crowd felt like one conjoined mass of emotion and praise and power. We were seeing this all happen together, in one place. It was the best night ever in rock-and-roll history. Ever! My best friends and I had seen it together, and we just knew then that nothing again in our lives could ever touch this experience we just had.

We were wrong.

Nothing had ever come close to that night until the Seahawks met the 49ers that day.

There was a weird smoke over the field for the whole game, not unlike that Zeppelin show. The crowd at that game, like that Zeppelin gig at the Dome, was truly anxious for what was to come and completely and unbelievably rowdy when it arrived.

Seattle has had a tough run as a professional sports town. We didn't even have the NFL or MLB until '76, and our 1979 Seattle Supersonics brought us our one and only championship trophy.

In the '70s and '80s, to the rest of the country, Seattle was "that little town up there somewhere." All we had was Boeing. Microsoft, Starbucks, Amazon, and grunge music helped expose the region to the rest of the world. Sports, however, remained veritably nonexistent in national media.

I think we like it that way. Seattleites are different. The 12th Man ethic, I believe, came about because, hell, if no one else was going to pay attention to the Seahawks, screw 'em! The fans would appreciate and support this team all by themselves.

And that's what we did on Sunday, January 19, 2014. We got behind our Hawks as they took the field, cheered louder than a jumbo jet when they fell behind at the half, and made some ears bleed as our team came from behind in the fourth quarter to give us another shot at winning the Super Bowl.

Special season, indeed.

SEE SOMETHING, SAY SOMETHING

T HE HAWKS' WIN MEANT TWO THINGS:

1. I was going to be celebrating my fiftieth birthday in New York, with my Seahawks in contention for the world championship.
2. We really needed tickets.

Jerry and I immediately went into a mad scramble to get tickets to, yes, the Super Bowl. We were finally willing to utter the word. Finding a place to stay was easy, and getting plane tickets was a breeze. But getting through the gate proved to be a bit harder. Paying $8,000 a ticket on StubHub was not going to happen (not when you've got two daughters in private school. Plus, who buys those tickets? Corporate accounts, right?).

I had a connection with an NFL executive back in '06 when we got excellent seats at face value. When I found out the exec was no longer with the NFL, I went back to square one. We'd figure it out. Somehow.

After the high of that momentous win over the 49ers, I began to feel well enough to get back into the gym. Sure, I was weak as hell, and nine weeks in bed had caused a few muscles to atrophy a bit, but I was back. When you train hard at my age, you get familiar with the sundry aches and pains in different parts of the body. People like us will sacrifice our bodies to pain and injury in the constant physical pursuit of mental ease and confidence. Even spiritual heights and clarity can be sought this way. It turns out there was an upside to being forced to lie prone for weeks on end: the time off my feet did wonders for my various joint aches. I took note that more days of rest should be in my future.

But not now, I thought: I'm gonna turn fifty! And my Seahawks are going to the SUPER BOWL! I'll rest later. There was work to do. Jerry and I—guys who didn't dare bring up the words "SUPER" or "BOWL" during the season—had been hell-bent on finding tickets from the moment the clock ticked to 00.00 during the NFC championship game. We were headed to New Jersey, and we were going to the game.

The reality of the Seattle Seahawks making it to the game of all games set the 12th Man and the entire city of Seattle on fire. The exaltation we felt as a city that week morphed into a sort of quiet confidence. I don't think the rest of the country gave the Hawks much of a chance against Peyton

Manning and his lofty squad of receivers. They were "destined." We were "upstarts."

I was really fortunate to have been able to write about my ticket search on NFL.com that week. A direct result of my quasi-public search for seats to the game was that a friend of mine who works for a guitar string company knew a guy who used to work at the Staples Center, and he called a friend of his who works for an NFL franchise who knew a guy in NFL ticketing who knew where to get a direct line on face-value tickets (got that?). All of this resulted in my pals and I getting some pretty kick-ass tickets. It kind of reminded me of long-past days of conducting shady deals and waiting by the phone for "the man" to call. Supply-and-demand economics in its rawest form.

Back in Los Angeles later that week, I'd been wearing my Seahawks baseball cap everywhere. At any other time of the year, it would have been just another hat. Just another team. But with the Super Bowl coming up, the hat became much more than just some other team's insignia. It became an indicator of what other people thought of my team.

My doctor told me he was sorry (already) for the brutal beating we were sure to take in New Jersey. I disagreed rather strongly and politely, but my ire was officially up. I went to the *Jimmy Kimmel Live* show to watch my buddy and fellow Seahawks fan Nikki Sixx and his band, Mötley Crüe, announce their Final Tour. It was a free, outside gig, hence there were a ton of people there.

"Seahawks suuuck!" was one young rocker's exclamation to my proudly worn colors. I, once again, soundly disagreed. (I think I went highbrow with a "YOU suck!" retort. You know, keeping it classy.)

After *Kimmel*, I called Tim Medvetz, a longtime pal you might know as the "biker" who was featured on Discovery Channel's *Everest: Beyond the Limit*.

Tim leads a profound life. His main mission these days is getting young amputee US servicemen and servicewomen up the biggest mountains on the planet. He raises the money and trains these young soldiers on his own. But Tim is also a proud New Jerseyite and was more than a little pissed about how the Super Bowl was being labeled the "New York/New Jersey Super Bowl."

"I mean, what the hell!?!?!" Tim said. "The Jets play in New Jersey, and they are called the New York Jets. The Giants play in New Jersey, and they are the New York Giants. The Super Bowl is in East Rutherford, NEW JERSEY, and they are calling this thing the 'New York/New Jersey Super Bowl!'"

Tim was just getting started: "And, they didn't even ask the Boss or Bon Jovi to play halftime!" A conversation with Tim always seems to end up at the Boss or Bon Jovi, no matter what the initial subject matter is. Kind of like us Seattleites, where the conversation always ends up with Jimi Hendrix or coffee or the Sonics getting stolen from our city. Or the 2013 Seahawks.

Jerry and I did a video feature for NFL Network about our support for the Hawks. The interviewer asked us both what it felt like to have our team looked at by the rest of the country as the bad guys. I guess I hadn't thought about that at all. The Seahawks are the bad guys? All right. Even that prospect felt OK with the both of us. We'll take it any way we can.

The Broncos, even for us Seahawks fans, were nearly impossible to vilify. Peyton Manning was the golden boy of destiny, and a large part of the rest of that team was made up of beloved veterans. We Seahawks are punk rock, and they are classic rock. But, remember, without punk rock actually shaking things up in the late 1970s, classic rock would have gone further and further into mellowsville. It would have died a slow death of gluttony. The Seattle Seahawks have shaken up how the NFL game is played, and it is fun to watch as your team is at the forefront of something new and exciting.

At the time, an old friend of mine was just moving to Manhattan's West Village. The place was all set up with furniture and beds, but he wasn't staying there yet. He offered the place to me and Jerry and my buddy Ed to crash during the Super Bowl—and my fiftieth. There you go. We wouldn't have to compete with all of the other Super Bowl–bound folks for a hotel room. We packed our cold-weather clothes and got a Friday Jet Blue flight to JFK. This was it!

The location of the seats we got for the game was still a mystery for us until just before our flight. We knew we'd be somewhere in the lower bowl of the stadium and were told that every seat down in that bowl had a great view. The tickets arrived via FedEx just before we left for the airport. Quickly checking the aisle and seat number against a stadium schematic that Jerry pulled up on his iPhone, we saw that we were in a veritable "position A." Our seats were in the fourth row, directly behind the Seahawks bench. This escalated our excitement, to put it mildly.

After landing at JFK, we headed into the city. The NFL Network had set us up to go to some party thing that we were only half interested in. Since the event was only four blocks from the place we were staying, we decided to wander up there after dropping our bags off at my buddy's pad in the Village.

There was a long line outside the party, and, after waiting in it for fifteen minutes or so (and the line not moving at all), we went around to the side VIP entrance to see if our names were there. "Yeah, you are on the list, guys, but we are just letting girls in now. No dudes. Just chicks."

Oh. We really didn't care. After all, we were in town for the game, not some dumb party. But for the rest of the weekend, the "no dudes, just chicks" saying became our mantra every time we got frustrated for dinner reservations or were faced with long lines at the myriad Super Bowl events we went to over the next forty-eight hours. Just when you think that maybe the "Duff from Guns N' Roses" tag or the "Jerry from Alice in Chains" handle can open doors, reality has a way of keeping one humble. I mean, seriously, my life at home with a wife and two daughters is a constant NO DUDES, JUST CHICKS affair. I don't need some beefy doorman to tell me that!

It was supposed to be really cold in the Northeast that weekend, and every face on television was trumpeting how the championship game would be affected by single-digit temperatures and the expected snowstorm. I was worried about my health in those temperatures and brought just about every layer of mountain gear I had. Mountain gear is really not meant for a fashionable place such as Manhattan. As a result, I was the only one in the fashionable West Village dressed ready to summit a 14,000-foot mountain. Fuck it. I ain't gettin' sick again, and this week was about football, not haute couture.

There is an important feature that binds Ed, me, and Jerry together besides our love of the Seahawks: all three of us are clean. Finally. The three of us all came very close to the edge with our consumption of alcohol and drugs, and we've survived a bunch of our fallen comrades. This point wasn't lost on us, and the simple fact that we have each lived long enough to finally be at this 2014 championship game, following the team through a bunch of our personally dark years, was not taken lightly. We've each had each other's backs through this fight and have been there to help others, as others have helped each one of us in the past. It's a cyclical and ongoing thing, being clean.

The place we were staying at in the West Village was on a tiny street with very little car traffic. The din of the big city seemed miles away. On Saturday, we had plans to go to Times Square to see Super Bowl Lane. We were going to go see the Foo Fighters later that night and maybe get some Super Bowl T-shirts for friends and family back home. Exiting the apartment, we ran smack-dab into a very famous actor. Being as this was an almost private street, we simply nodded to him and kept on our way, not wanting to intrude on his private life. Ed commented that the actor had been clean for something like twenty-three years, but he'd heard that he'd recently started using again. Should we turn around and offer to take the guy for a coffee? As I said, keeping sober is a group effort. We trudged on through the cold, discussing the matter.

Later that afternoon when we came back, we saw the actor in the street again and could tell that he was waiting to score. Should we offer our friendship and a safe place? This is sometimes the dilemma for sober guys—as we all know, you can't force a guy to get sober. He has to come around to it himself. We went back into the apartment.

Later that night, before the Foo Fighters show, the three of us were hanging out in a backstage green room with a bunch of music industry folks and whatnot, when a couple of security guys came in and cleared the room. But they told the three of us we could stay. We assumed that because we are actual friends with the guys in the Foos, they were just clearing out everyone else so that the band could pass through the room, hassle-free, on the way to the stage. Suddenly, two bigger security guys came through with none other than Sir Paul McCartney. We "no dudes, just chicks" guys were good enough, apparently, to be trusted in such small confines with a fucking Beatle!

"Hi, Duff! Hi, Jerry! How's it going, guys?" Pretty good, Paul . . . pretty good. And yeah, screw those dudes over at that other VIP line from the night before! All was suddenly right in the world. Our Seahawks would be on the world's biggest football stage the next day, and Paul goddamned Mc-Cartney knew me and Jerry by name! No dudes! Just chicks!

After the show, we were visibly giddy about the game, which was only a few hours away. We took a cab back down to the apartment and got dropped off in front of the place at about 1:30 a.m. We ran smack-dab into the actor again. On the street. Waiting. Again. Shit, man. We thought that maybe he was on a last run before getting clean. Surely if we saw him again in the morning, we'd have to say something.

Bro, c'mon. We've been there. Come on out of the cold. We understand. We've been there. Really. We've been there.

The next morning—Sunday, February 2, 2014, the morning of the Super Bowl—I heard a ruckus outside our front door. I went out to take a look. There was an ambulance and police, and a whole crowd of press people and fans. The actor had OD'd and died sometime after we saw him at 1:30 a.m. the night before. (Out of respect for his children and our joint association with a "fraternity," I don't feel comfortable calling him out by name.)

The three of us gathered in the kitchen of our apartment. We were stunned. I've been through this before with friends, and friends of friends, but I'll never get used to it. Sure, none of us knew the actor personally, but he was one of us. The three of us understood that we could, at any time, be just one small and easy step from being the guy out there on the street waiting for the dealer to show. When guys like us witness something like this go down, it makes you take stock of where you are at in your sobriety.

We'd been following this Seattle team since we were twelve years old. Ed has OD'd countless times and shouldn't be here. Jerry abused himself so badly that here was a point in his life when he didn't care if he lived or died. My pancreas burst at thirty, and here I was three days away from turning fifty. We'd all lost close friends to this thing, but we'd survived. It may seem trite, but it was so heavy to us that we were going to be able to celebrate our team at the Super Bowl later that day. The actuality of the three of us still drawing breath, living long enough to witness this day, was profound at that moment. A great actor's sudden death drove the point home.

There was nothing left for us to do. We shook hands and looked toward the stadium. The game became even more of a thing for me. In my private thoughts, I was proud of Jerry and Ed, and grateful that I made it, too. I was grateful to have a family of girls who look to me at times for guidance and security and comfort. As our car eased into the parking lot of Giants Stadium, my stomach churned with so many emotions.

Our team came to New York so ready to play and tore the unsuspecting Denver Broncos to shreds. We stood in the stands and didn't let our guard down—or even breathe—until that game was over and we were Super Bowl champions at long last. It was really quite unbelievable for us

Seattle fans. The underdog city, the underdog team, and I think we three dudes felt like the underdogs who had survived when many betted against us in the past.

It was a victory, to be sure. But there was something bittersweet about it. Thinking about the great actor, his final day, and being among the last people to see him alive reminded me that I'd been here before.

I was on an LA-SEA flight with Kurt Cobain in 1994. We were both fucked up. We talked, but not in-depth. I was in my hell, and he in his. This, we both seemed to understand.

When we arrived in Seattle and went to baggage claim, the thought crossed my mind to invite him over to my house. I had a real sense that he was lonely and alone that night. I felt the same way. There was a mad rush of people there in public. I was in a big rock band. He was in a big rock band. We were standing next to each other. Lots of people stopped to gawk. I lost my train of thought for a minute, and Kurt said good-bye and left to his waiting town car. His new house was right down the street from my new house. A few days later, I received a call from my manager, who told me that Kurt had committed suicide.

After the game, I thought about my daughters, my beautiful wife, my friends, and my bandmates. My life was overflowing with gifts. At thirty, my doctors didn't think I'd make it to thirty-one. I wasn't supposed to.

But, here I was, twenty years later, with friends, celebrating victory for our Seahawks, and being ever more grateful that we'd been given a second chance.

DON'T DIE YOUNG, YOU'LL MISS OUT ON BEING FIFTY

IN THE LATE '80S AND '90S, THERE WAS A MESS OF drug-addled youth in their twenties in and around rock-and-roll music who bought into the "Live Fast, Die Young" mantra and all its accompanying rot. My friends and I were squarely among this misguided camp who believed it. It's amazing that, even today, after everything we've been through, after all of the obituaries and unfinished business, you still read about artists admirably described as being "elegantly wasted."

My time as a teenage musician in Seattle coincided with an influx of wave upon wave of heroin in the port city we called home. The person who personifies the era best to me was a young man with a hopeful glint in his eye and so much more. He was one of the funniest and most charming guys I've ever met. His name was Chris Harvey, but everyone called him Slats.

Slats and I did not have a boat. But he had a car.

On the southern border of the University of Washington campus lies its school of aquatic and fishery sciences and its salmon hatchery. Slats thought it a brilliant idea for us to hop the fence with a bucket and scoop up salmon so we could clean 'em, freeze 'em, and eat 'em for weeks. Everything worked according to plan, and we had a bunch of flopping salmon in a big bucket when the floodlights went on and the night watchman came chasing after us.

I told Slats to just drop the bucket, but he was having none of it. He managed to scale the fence with that damn thing in his hand. One of the funniest memories I will ever have is of him driving the car back to my apartment with his left hand on the wheel while punching the flopping salmon with his right. He had a running commentary with those fish all the way home, saying they almost got us into big trouble and now they would pay the ultimate price.

I loved that guy like a brother, once upon a time, back when the playing field of youth was even and green and soft and we were just opening our eyes to what was possible in life. He was the one the rest of us wanted to be like. He had the good looks and charm that all the girls fawned over. He never gloated or preened in his status as the coolest guy in the room, and that very thing made him even cooler.

I'm not sure how or when I initially met Slats, but it must have been sometime in 1980, when we were both either in bands or trying to start one. After we met, though, we became fast and all-of-the-time friends. We started our first band, the Zipdads, together with Andy Freeze from the Vains and Scott Dittman from the Cheaters.

The Zipdads were really more a lifestyle than a musical statement. Sure, we played a bunch of shows in Seattle and Vancouver, British Columbia, but it was the fun we had together that really set us apart and was the thing other people and bands wanted to be a part of. Slats was always the instigator at the center of the fun.

His mom, too, was so supportive of her son and would regularly have us all over for dinner at their home. We would pick up his Gibson SG and Fender amp, and he would always speak highly of his mom even after we left the house. Most teenage boys would find SOMETHING to gripe on their parents about, but not Slats. I always admired that.

When we went out, he always had the smoothest of smooth one-liners for girls. I had no idea where he accumulated his vast repertoire—maybe he just made that shit up on the spot—but girls fell for it hook, line, and sinker (he was a fisherman after all, right?).

Slats never was one of the most skilled guitar players, but he crafted his own sound back in our day. When he formed the Silly Killers in 1982, his sound and sense of songwriting were really starting to take shape. Their 7-inch single, "Knife Manual," is a classic. I don't think it was too much later that he started to dabble with heroin. He never found his musical form again, and that is sad. Slats died a couple years ago, of complications due to a broken hip. Unfortunately, the drugs claimed him long before, and he never broke free.

I had seen him around at Loaded shows and elsewhere over the past ten years but always tried to avoid him because our paths had grown too far apart. Frankly, I was dubious and protective of my life. I wasn't being a good friend. To be honest, I don't know what we would have had to talk about. But I could have tried. I should have tried.

Turning fifty years of age is a milestone. For many, it's terrifying, an "oh, shit!" moment that one dreads. Me, I was rather relieved and more than a little elated. Guys like me were not supposed to get here. But here I am, on the healthy side of life. A little wiser, I suppose. My left ankle hurts in the morning. But my inner thoughts and aspirations remain the same as when I was nine years old. When the body have walked as many miles as you do when you've been on this planet for this long, it doesn't mean your mind and outlook really change. Mine didn't.

I keep hearing that fifty is the new thirty, thanks to modern medicine. Some say it's because our diet and water have gotten better, that we've become more health conscious. We moisturize our skin, use sunscreen, and look after ourselves better than our parents did. We have more sex. There are more gyms. More ways to keep the body and mind healthy and satisfied.

I'm not buying any of it.

I believe we're staying young longer because of rock and roll. Because of the generation that decided they weren't going to die before they got old. Instead of dying young, they just didn't get old. Fifty is the new thirty—or, twenty-nine, really—because the Rolling Stones, Aerosmith, Iggy, and Motörhead keep touring. They provide a template for the rest of us. They show us how good, how seasoned we get as we age. They show us how many good times can be had after our forties.

The trick to staying young in any era—and in any profession and relationship—is to have something to strive for. I've seen Aerosmith many times since the *Rocks* tour, and every time you can just tell that they are pushing themselves to play that perfect show.

We all have our down moments. We all have that thing in the middle of the night that my mom used to call the "3 a.m. blues." You can't always kick ass. I'd be a liar if I said I was batting anywhere close to a thousand. But you have to try. You have to recognize the times when you're falling down and pick yourself back up. For me, that means going to see Motörhead, Iggy, and Aerosmith—guys who have saved my butt time and again.

Aerosmith have somehow kept themselves current and relevant through countless fads and eras in rock and pop music, and they do it by constantly writing songs. They definitely have that "thing" to strive for, and they are, at seventeen or more years older than me, ageless.

The Stones are almost a generation older (in age, that is) than the boys in Aerosmith. But they were still filming high-definition concert films during their 50th Anniversary

Tour. We in the audience can see the creases, scars, warts, and all. They don't give a fuck, and they are a quarter of a century older than I am. I'd be an asshole at this point to think fifty was anywhere close to old. The Stones have single-handedly raised the worldwide bar of how we, as men, think about ourselves in terms of age.

I met a guy the other day, and we immediately began to talk about our kids (of course). When we both figured out that our kids were basically the same age, I almost said to him: "Wow, you must have had your kids when you were in your late forties!" I'm so glad I didn't. This fella not only looked to be sixty-six or older, but he acted as if he had given up on life. You could tell that he told himself, every day, that he was old. I was shocked when he told me he was fifty-two.

That moment was a quick one, but it scared me. It reminded me of what can happen when a man gives up, when he doesn't have something to shoot for, when he continues to pine for his twenty-third birthday. I saw what could happen if a guy just gives up. Later that night, I went and saw Aerosmith, and I was once again saved not only by their music but by the guys playing it. They shook me free of that experience earlier in the day.

And Iggy, Lemmy? These fellas run nonstop. I know for a fact that Lemmy enjoys touring today as much as he ever has. Motörhead keeps putting out bigger and better records, and Iggy reinvigorated the Stooges after taking, oh, thirty years away from it to focus on a solo career that personified

striving for something new and different and musically challenging. All of these people are straight-up living, and striving, looking aggressively beyond fifty. (And I haven't even
started talking about Prince!)

I love being fifty. It's a wonderful gift. On my birthday, I
thought about my daughters, my wife, and the friends who
have walked me through the hard times and been with me
during the good times when we could act like kids and cry
for our Seahawks.

I thought about Kurt, I thought about the actor in the
West Village, and I thought about Slats. I was so sad that
they weren't going to know what it felt like to be fifty, to see
their team win and their daughters grown, and to become
the men that they were capable of becoming.

There's nothing elegant about being wasted. There isn't
nobility in dying before you get old.

INNOVATE AND MODERNIZE.
THEN GET UP AND DO IT AGAIN

F INALLY FIFTY AND HOME FROM THE SUPER BOWL, I took the opportunity to have a look at the Walking Papers' receipts for 2013. We'd spent the year touring, promoting our self-titled debut record. We'd been all across the United States and through Europe twice and driven more miles than I care to count (and still had a few dates in Australia on the horizon). Through it all, we sold 20,000 copies of our album. Roughly 15,000 of those were sold by a member of the band at our merch table, where we shook hands, took selfies, and thanked fans for supporting us.

We worked with a record label, but, as you can see, we sold most of our records on our own. That counts for something. We went most of the year in the red, sure, but we landed a nice New Year's Eve gig in Seattle that pushed us

into the black. Running at breakeven means the band is going to be able to make another record. And now that we've
shown we can move units and draw crowds, labels with
more power and exposure to broader markets are knocking
on our door. We're also getting offers for serious headlining
dates in Europe.

While 20,000 units may not seem like much, by today's
standards, it's more than respectable.

When I toured Europe with GN'R in the early '90s, we
could afford to lose money on the road and use the shows as
a loss leader to sell records. It was a traveling advertisement
to sell a stationary product in record stores.

It's not like that anymore. No one is selling records like
they used to. In the United States, 785 million albums were
sold in 2000, and the best-selling album of the year, N'Sync's
No Strings Attached, moved 9.9 million units. In 2013, 415
million albums were sold. The best-selling album, former
N'Sync front man Justin Timberlake's *The 20/20 Experience,* moved 3 million units. (If you think album sales are
down because of quality, are you really going to try and argue that *Strings* is better than *20/20?* I didn't think so.)

I am in a unique position to observe all of this change
in the music business, for three reasons: (1) I came from a
punk rock DIY "fuck the man" beginning. (2) After playing in
many punk rock bands, I moved to Los Angeles and formed
the ultimate "fuck the man" band that became so successful
that I've been able to form more "fuck the man" bands. (3) I
formed a new band (Velvet Revolver) with former members

of my old band, sold a good amount of records, *and* sold a lot of concert tickets.

With Velvet Revolver, we could see the change in the industry. No one was selling records like they used to, thanks to file sharing.

It can get goofy when I talk about how file sharing has made things difficult for struggling and developing artists. I wrote a fairly open-minded piece for *Seattle Weekly* a couple of years ago that fetched hundreds of comments, most of them squarely in the "shut up, rock star" vein. It's alright. I can take it. But it leaves me scratching my head when, in trying to prop up new music and the overall survival of new music as a whole, a guy like me will take critical shots.

People just don't wanna pay for music anymore. That's the bottom line. Okay. But if you want to see your favorite band continue to make new music, buy the album. And if you want to see your favorite band continue to tour, at least go out and see the show—and pick up a T-shirt or piece of vinyl so the band can put gas in their van and breakfast in their bellies. Get your friends into the band and bring them along. It has almost gone all the way back to 1980, when we were folding single sleeves in the front living room of a punk-rock house. New rock music is almost all DIY, so as fans we have to step up. As artists, we have to do everything we can to adapt.

With Velvet Revolver, we pared back our touring costs, and I looked deeper than I ever had into T-shirt printing prices and how we could offer other apparel that fans were willing to buy. We started to do VIP ticket packages in 2004 because we knew that if we wanted to survive and even thrive in this new paradigm, we'd have to do things that we never had to do before. As an artist working through these changes, I've been at the front lines of adapting to the new realities. Companies that don't adapt to change and modernization will wither and cease to exist. I'm not about to cease to exist. Hell, I haven't even *started* yet.

All a band can really hope for these days is to get their record distributed widely enough to get enough exposure for the band that people will know who they are and maybe then come to one of their shows—and buy a record. This is how you build your business in music these days. And even in this digital age, when everyone's got iTunes and Spotify, if a band's CDs don't arrive, the results can be catastrophic.

A few years ago, Loaded was playing the Sweden Rock Festival in Malmo, promoting a new record for a record company we had just gone into business with. The record company had made assurances that they'd have our product in stores in the cities and towns we'd be touring in and that they'd do some promotion with magazines and websites in those areas as well. Getting these assurances was important, as we had experienced on our previous record a completely botched record-selling campaign in which we'd toured the world and our records were not available anywhere we played. Not one. It was beyond maddening.

The new company was not doing much better, but we had just started with them, and we were in constant communication with them about how they could better their exposure with us out there. Sweden Rock Festival has a really cool setup where they have an actual record store on the premises, with records and CDs available from all seventy artists playing the three-day event. Not only that but each band gets a two-hour signing window at the store. The customer must buy a CD or record to get a signature, and fans in Malmo have never had a problem buying records.

Our record company was on us big time to make the signing. "Of COURSE, we will!" I said. They promised the records would be there the night before. They didn't show. Then they said they'd be there first thing in the morning, which was fine because our signing wasn't until 1 p.m. We assumed everything would be cool. Since the band had never been to Sweden, our line was almost a thousand people deep by the time we showed up. We were all pretty damn surprised. That's a thousand records sold, to say nothing of the friends that they'd go home and play the record for, and the ancillary sales that would explode from the signing. Of course . . . our records never showed up.

When I was growing up, just putting out a 7-inch single was a massive deal. In those innocent punk-rock days, we'd work two jobs just to pay for some shitty gear and a shitty place to rehearse. One of our friends would design the sleeve for the single. We'd bring it to the printer, print huge glossy sheets of album art, and go home and have a cut-and-paste party. The next day at school, we'd nick the key to the copy room and make a bunch of black-and-white copies of the artwork for the next batch of albums—also created at a cut-and-paste party. Pasting together sleeves for my own single was one of the coolest things I ever got to do, because it meant that I had a *record* coming out!

I try not to forget those early, halcyon days of my music career. In all of the talk about music being shared, the business side of things has totally changed. But those of us who have been around for a while remember those old days when it was just cool to have something of your own out in the *first* place.

But it's not enough just to have a record out anymore. This has become my career. I'm a working dad. I have a family that depends upon my income. This is where things like having no product available—or fans downloading albums without paying for them—can get irksome. I still *think* punk rock, but these days I have to work a real payday into the equation. We all do.

But, until we find some other model for making and distributing records, this old way of getting physical records distributed to areas an artist is playing struggles on. I'm not pointing my finger at anyone. Most labels are smaller these days and are barely able to survive. The larger labels have, for the most part, had to depend on ultracommercial pop music marketed to young kids (and their parents, who will willingly buy music for their little darlings). The major labels these days can't afford to take a risk to develop great rock music.

It's easy to think of a band like U2 as always having been a colossus—and for fans born in the '90s, they always have been. But Island Records stuck with the band for four albums before they broke with *Joshua Tree*. Labels today don't have the resources to do that anymore. Sometimes I think about how many U2s have broken up this year or last because they just couldn't sell enough records to make a follow-up. It's not that they don't love making music anymore. It's that they have to feed their kids.

The Walking Papers are a musical powerhouse. I'm not saying that because I am in the band. I joined this thing because of how much respect I have for the guys who started the band. Jeff Angell and Barrett Martin are two of the most creative guys I've ever worked with. And keyboard-ist Ben Anderson's approach to auxiliary sound is sublime. This band is just one example of a group that could de-velop into something special (on the road, we see others all the time). Of course, we need to keep selling records to continue. We've all got kids and homes and responsibilities now. Those cute old punk-rock days of just being excited to have a 7-inch out have been supplanted by hard facts. We *have* to financially succeed to a degree in selling product if we are going to continue this band. This *is* our job now: to create a place where our kids can record and wrap 7-inch singles of their own.

It is a much tougher row to hoe these days to break your band, but goddamn, it's still all about the music. Playing our songs, writing new ones, and imagining what could be, it all feels the same as it did when I was sixteen years old.

I can't wait to do it all again.

KNOW HOW THINGS WORK (AND WHAT YOU CAN FIX)

"To make mistakes is human; to stumble is commonplace; to be able to laugh at yourself is maturity."
—WILLIAM ARTHUR WARD

W HEN I'M HOME, LIFE IS PRETTY NORMAL AROUND
the McKagan house: my daughters go to school
during the day and spend evenings in their rooms (I thought
we were over this!); Susan and I spend our days talking about
our girls and our evenings worrying about them. I try to fix
things around the house. I like to fix things. Always have.

I bought my first car when I was seventeen. I had a
steady job as a cook in Seattle and saved up enough money
to spend three hundred dollars on a ride. That was a lot
of money in 1982, especially for a guy barely making four
dollars an hour—who had rent to pay. I wasn't old enough

to legally buy a car, so, like I had done a few times before, I asked Kim Warnick from the Fastbacks to be my adult representative. At nineteen, she was an adult in the eyes of the law and fit to cosign for the car.

I found a Ford Maverick with 200,000 miles on it, but the owner explained to me that "that slant-six engine would run for another 200,000!" He also said something as an aside about the car being able to make it to LA without a problem. That was all the confidence I needed to drive to LA and find some guys to start a band with. He could never know what an impact on my life that sentence would have.

While, yes, the engine may have been fine, I soon learned that the brakes weren't. The brakes were spongy, and after a week I had to start applying the brakes a good half block before red lights and stop signs. I explained the situation to the guy working the counter at a local auto parts store. Considering my limited funds, he pointed me toward a junkyard north of Seattle to look for something called a master cylinder. I had never seen a master cylinder before and soon found out that they are massive, daunting objects.

The junkyard was filled with rows and rows of towering hunks of rust and rubber: cars stacked on top of cars, all with scribbled codes in different colors of ink. I found out that the different colors signified different intentions: yellow meant that the engine was intact, blue signified that the body parts were in good shape. I had to go to the main office at the junkyard a few times to finally find an area at the yard where I might find what I was looking for. The guys in the office seemed to take an interest in my case and, sensing that I was a complete neophyte, started doling out advice. I even managed to learn a few things.

While tearing a master cylinder out of one car, I figured out how the bolts worked for when I'd have to install it back into my car. But, really, I didn't know what I was doing. I didn't know, for example, that one had to bleed the brake lines of their fluid and keep vacuum pressure before installation. I failed. Three times. After each attempt I made my way back to the junkyard, to the boys in the office, asking the gruff dudes at the yard for advice. I still don't pretend to know how a car's brake system works, but I did figure out my Maverick. The whole process taught me about patience and trying to ask more questions and get more informed BEFORE I had the next issue with my car—or anything else for that matter.

I like to know how the stuff around me works. I know that a light doesn't just automatically turn on when you flip a switch. There is power running from the street to your house and then fuses and conduits and whatnot. That power from the street comes from some sort of city power plant, where that electrical energy was converted from a dam somewhere and transported all the way to your light switch.

It's fun to learn how inanimate objects—broken lighting sconces, brick walkways, undug trenches, and unlayed sprinklers—work. And it's fun to figure out how to fix them.

It's in our blood. Men like to fix things. Sometimes out of necessity—and sometimes because we can't sit still.

Sometimes because we're in a position to fix things. And others, um, because we mean well. We try to fix our cars, our toilets, even our relationships. We can't help it. We try to fix things. But there are things we can't fix.

Our twenties and thirties can be a real pain in the ass. A lot of us think that by that age we *must* have it all figured out. The fact is that learning about ourselves and others is not static; it's an ever-changing process.

When I have problems or confusions with my wife and loved ones, it's easy to forget that I'm only seeing the light switch. When we fellas try to fix a problem in our relationships, we naturally want the immediate malaise to be cured. We try patching things up without thinking of *where* the current of the problem with our loved one is coming from. The street, the city power plant, or the dam? I'm not a pop psychologist of any sort, but I've found that trying to look a little deeper and trying to understand the *whole* situation with my wife or daughters goes a lot further for both parties involved.

Teenage kids spend a ton of time in their rooms. They have iPads and iPhones and Spotify, and my wife and I have gotten used to our daughters going straight to their rooms after school. But when I hear a door *slam* when one of them comes home from school, I know there is something wrong. My first reaction, instinctively, is to scold her for slamming the door shut, but I've come to realize that this is only the light switch to some *other* situation that my daughter may be having.

These days there are a few more variables than a dam and a city power plant and a fuse. With teenagers, there is school, girlfriends, boys, social media, driving, college pressure, and, yes, us parents. Peeling back the onion can be challenging with a teenager, but I hope that by gently prodding and eventually getting to the root of an issue, my girls will soon enough learn a little about exposing their own problems to themselves and self-solving. Hell, these kids grow up so damn fast that before you know it, they will be out on their own.

Back when Susan was having our babies, she started making a habit of showing me different clothes she liked in magazines and catalogues we got in the mail. I was busy in school and studied for hours at home each day when I wasn't physically at school. I'd feign interest when she showed me a pashmina or dress from a catalogue, or, when we were out to dinner, and she'd point out something in a store window. Me being a guy, I simply would go get her these things from the mall or downtown on the way home from school, thinking this would fix the issue. Right? Wrong.

When I'd bring something home for her, she'd sort of half smile, say thanks, and leave the item where it sat for a week. This started to bug me as much as it was seemingly bothering her. I couldn't figure it out. Finally, one night we got into a little spat. That's when I finally found out why I was getting the "gift-clothes" cold shoulder. What I wasn't noticing when she'd show me those clothes in magazines was that she wanted us to go together and look for that beige pashmina at Nordstrom. In my rush to fill my brain with knowledge at the business school at Seattle U, I was forgetting that my wife liked to spend time with me, too. It could have been clothes she was pointing out to me or vegetables from the grocery store mailer. She just wanted us to do some small things together. Duh.

I don't know the whole story with friends or strangers who are short with me at the gym, either. I try to talk to people and learn from others, and I realize most of the time that I just can't go back to some scrapyard and get another part when it comes to relationships. The overarching male intuition to fix has to be pushed back for us boys if we're ever to grow into bona fide man-dom.

LET GO OF RESENTMENTS, VOL. I

"Mountaintops inspire leaders,
but valleys mature them."
—SIR WINSTON CHURCHILL

THIS, I WAS NOT EXPECTING. I GUESS THAT'S THE POINT.
When I was thirty, I believed that if I made it to fifty my life would have a straight path forward, that I'd know exactly how every day was going to end. Every year since, I've been further convinced I was wrong.

I have much more at fifty than I ever imagined I would. Only through adaptation and change have I been able to enjoy the process. My daughters are more than any father could ask for, and my marriage is still spicy.

(Note: To you young married couples. There is no such thing, I believe, as a marriage without conflict. The important thing in all relationships is to get rid of resentments. Resentment will absolutely kill any relationship.)

A couple months after my birthday, I was in Australia with the Walking Papers. We were offered a great spot on the touring Soundwave Festival, playing seven shows in five cities, and things were going pretty swell. Susan was with me, and the girls were in the midst of schoolwork back home. They were happy to get a break from their parents, and Susan and I were having some serious grown-up time in a fantastic part of the world.

(Note to married couples with children: Grown-up time is very important. Getting away from the kids for a night or more and wearing fancy underwear—guys—is healthy all the way around.)

Out of nowhere, I got a call from a good friend who has been working for Axl. He told me that there was a scheduling mix-up and that GN'R's bass player, Tommy Stinson, couldn't play some South American dates with the band. "The gigs are booked and tickets are on sale. Duff, could you come down and play them with Axl and the guys?"

It had been seventeen years since I'd played many of those songs. In those seventeen years, a lot of chest puffing and resentment building had taken place. That band was such a monstrous thing that none of us original guys were able to walk away unscathed. I'd done things that I wasn't proud of. I'd had feelings about it that, looking back now, seem completely sophomoric.

Members of the GN'R inner circle said things about me, too, that I didn't appreciate. Being able to get through this stuff and work on resentments and figure out what my part in the whole thing was has been a healthy part of me getting the chance to mature, to not just appreciate but love all of the original guys from the band. We did a lot together in a short amount of time, and I realize how some of the dirty water that flowed under our bridge came to be muddied. Today, I look back at those times with something close to honor.

Of course, when you have kids, you don't have a lot of time to look back at life. Kids keep a guy in the now in a big way. Kids have diapers, bottles, and toys . . . toys that a dad has to put together. Kids have preschool, kindergarten, grade school, high school . . . and drama and boys. And more drama.

Dads go back to school. Dads start new business endeavors. Dads get sober, sharpen their minds with martial arts. Dads work on their marriage. Dads play fart tennis with their bandmates; write columns for *Seattle Weekly,* ESPN, and *Playboy;* and write books about dogs and how to keep roses alive in the backyard. We follow the Seahawks, say good-bye to the Sonics. We replace the blown lightbulbs in the motorcycle. We keep up with friends. I assumed life would slow down at fifty. It does not. Many of my formative years were spent elbow to elbow with the guys in GN'R. Axl and I had a great bond that I let bad advice and internal politics push me away from. Resentment reared its ugly head. This shit happens, and I'm glad I found a way out of that period. I've yet to find any good purpose for resentment anywhere in my life. As a friend once told me: resentment is like taking poison and hoping the other person gets sick.

This call from my friend was much more than a call about some gig. It was a chance to rectify mistakes and re-cover a friendship. But I had to think about it. I've gotten similar calls before.

Toward the end of 2011, just as Loaded was wrapping up a world tour, I got a call: would we open for Axl and GN'R in Seattle and Vancouver? I had to think of this several different ways: Would my band that's still trying to recruit new fans perform in front of 20,000 people predisposed to liking our music? Would I like to tack one more show onto the end of a grueling tour? Would I like to open for a band that's performing hits that I cowrote?

In the end, I decided, yes, we'd play the shows. Not only would it be a good chance to give Loaded a look at some new fans, but I'd have a chance to start the process of getting to know my friend again.

A few days before the show, my phone rang again: I was to be inducted into the Rock and Roll Hall of Fame as a member of Guns N' Roses. This news left me grateful—and speechless. It also cast the shows with Axl in a different light.

I'm so glad we played the shows. Not only was our set vicious, but I had a chance to sit in with Axl and his band. Seeing the way the crowd reacted to the sight of the two of us together reminded me of something: as big as GN'R was for me, my bandmates, and our families, it was bigger to our fans. It left a lasting impact that I don't think I'll ever be able to fully comprehend.

At the time, I felt like it could have been the beginning of a new chapter for me and Axl, and maybe even the whole band. We were to be honored with an induction into the Rock and Roll Hall of Fame. Perhaps it would be time for us to finally put the past behind us and move forward.

It wasn't meant to be. My friend Izzy Stradlin asked me to relay a message via my *Seattle Weekly* blog that he would not be attending the event. And Axl released his own letter soon after announcing his intention not to attend. I know both men had their reasons, but I couldn't help but feel like we were missing an opportunity and letting down our fans.

I received an open letter from a fan named Chris Gehrt on behalf of "Worldwide Guns N' Roses Fans" that put a sharp point on the situation:

Dear Guns N' Roses,

On Saturday April 14th 2012 you will be inducted into the Rock and Roll Hall of Fame. This gave a great hope to every GN'R fan on the planet for a one time reunion show. Our one and only chance to see the original lineup on stage together again, if only for five minutes. Something we've been told for years would never happen. Rumors swirled, the band denied, and the fans prayed. It will always be okay because you never promised us anything.

With less than 2 weeks before the induction, the fans are watching as our reunion hopes start to disappear like Marty McFly's family in a polaroid picture. Each day it seems like there is some new story about how there has been no communication, nobody knows what is required of them, nobody's talking, and nobody really seems to care.

We care.

It would be easy for you to just show up, accept the induction, spend a few awkward minutes together at a podium and not talk again until somebody's funeral. But this time we need more.

We are not trying to be selfish, God knows you have given us plenty of legendary songs, spectacular shows, and classic rock moments. You are sincerely the best rock band in the history of the world. All of your solo efforts and reincarnations of the group are awesome too.

Your music has inspired billions of people. Each one of you is still a fan inside. You loved Elton John, Aerosmith, Queen, Kiss, The Misfits, ELO and more. Please remember how great it feels to see your favorite band play.

We beg you to pick up the phone, grab your instruments, drag Izzy to Cleveland and play together.

You can make music history. Please do it. Give us one more memory. We deserve it.

We will continue to support you no matter what, but at the end of each concert Axl tells the crowd to "Not take . . . from anyone." And that means ANYONE!

Sincerely,
Worldwide Guns N' Roses Fans.

The letter was painful, but also inspiring. With Slash, Steven, Matt, and I all planning to attend, I knew we'd have to do something special for our fans. It all went by in such a blur that the details didn't come into focus until after I watched the performance on the HBO special weeks later.

It was a very poignant event. I don't think I was expecting just how heavy the whole deal was going to be for me on a personal level. Walking into the lobby at the hotel that all the artists were staying at, the first person I saw was fucking Ronnie Wood from the Faces/Stones. He gave me a huge hug and smiled a huge grin. "Isn't this going to be fucking great, Duff?!" Uh, yeah, sure . . . but, what a welcome it was.

In the aftermath of all of the drama leading up to the event, I stuck to my mind-set that I was there to honor our fan base who had been there for us over the last twenty-five years.

A funny thing happened in the lead-up to Cleveland. It seemed that there was an understanding not only with the people who flew in to Cleveland to see "their band" inducted but in how the other bands inducted rallied around Slash, Steven, Matt, and me. They had our backs, and all offered their help in any way that we could use it.

Flea gave me a big hug later that afternoon, and so did Chad Smith. You can always count on the Red Hot Chili Peppers. The Green Day guys came to my book reading the night before at the House of Blues. Billie Joe and I devised a plan for him to sing whatever was needed . . . if needed.

We really didn't know if we were going to play at all, and it wasn't cemented until we actually rehearsed at 2 a.m. the day of the show. We rehearsed with Steven Adler. Slash and I hadn't played those songs with him in something like twenty-two years. Would it work? Would we be able to get our mojo back with only fourteen hours before playing in front of an audience of 7,000, not to mention being filmed for an HBO special!?

We snagged Gilby Clarke and Myles Kennedy to come join us, and both guys killed it.

Watching the HBO special, I was struck by what an honor it was to have been included in such an epic class of bands and artists. GN'R had opened for the Chili Peppers a few times in LA in the early days. They were king shit on the hill back then. And the Beasties were the hard-core East Coast counterpart to what we were oozing over on the West Coast. I do seem to remember us both being in the same club sometime in 1986, and the rumor of us brawling against each other was rampant throughout the room that night. Ah, testosterone!

The Faces, by the way, are just in a whole and separate class from the rest of us young(ish) bucks. They are grand. They are class. They are . . . the Faces!

So, there we all were, bands that made a difference somewhere. I couldn't have been more proud of the guys I took the stage with that night. Those men composed themselves in light of so much unneeded drama. We had no resentment and showed up to pay homage to the fans who did their part for us.

Watching the HBO special made me sad—for the very first time, perhaps—that the original GN'R didn't somehow stay together. It would have been a miracle if we did. Had I known then what I know now, I would have done my part to try to rid that band of the caustic resentments and outside inputs that finally wore us down to a nub of what we once were.

But at the end of the day, I am so very satisfied about the outcome of that night in Cleveland. It was about the music that GN'R wrote way back when. And the fact that a few of us showed up to reciprocate our appreciation was certainly enough for that particular occasion.

Opening up for Axl's band and the Rock Hall induction wasn't enough to kick-start our friendship again. But as I considered his offer to join his band in South America, I thought: I'm 50, it's time for peace.

When I agreed to do the shows, I put my blinders on, blocking from view all of the outside opinions that came cascading my way. I only hoped that Axl and I would find a way to simply shake hands, honor the music we made, and, hopefully, flush away some of the past bad residue. This was an excellent opportunity for all of that, and I knew that I would have at least tried, no matter how it turned out. Trying for something is better that not trying.

My next step: trying to remember the songs!

LET GO OF RESENTMENTS, VOL. II

AFTER I AGREED TO PLAY THE SHOWS, I QUICKLY realized that I hadn't played many of these songs in a long, long time. Axl and I started to communicate, and our initial discourse—via text, naturally—reminded me of the levity that made up about 75 percent of our old relationship: knock-knock jokes. They're my specialty, really. But I was impressed to discover that Axl had amassed quite a catalogue of his own during our time apart.

I had to reach deep into my knock-knock war chest to keep up. But then our conversation turned to the songs, the real shit that mattered. It was a bit strange at first, the two of us texting about which GN'R songs we were gonna do. He and I hadn't had a conversation about a set list in like twenty years. Twenty years ago, there wasn't even texting!

"Estranged"? Oh, yeah . . . I love that song. "My Michelle"? Right. In F♯, I think. Killer! Just killer. "Think About You"? Shit! Old school! Yes! "November Rain"? Epic. The song list went on, through "Welcome to the Jungle" and "Sweet Child" and, yeah, just about everything. These were the songs that we sweated and bled for back in that magical time, when everything happened so quickly.

I realized there in my basement room, going through these songs again, just how fucking good we were. I'm not trying to blow smoke or be cute here, I just simply forgot how heavy that music is. It was a bit emotional. With those songs cranking through my ghetto blaster and my bass in my lap, I was transported back to a time when the fellowship and songwriting of that band was in its prime.

My bass-playing chops are, in most ways, much better and more refined than they were in 1987. I've played a lot over the past two decades, so how could it not be a little better, right? But I had to regress a bit and get back into the animalistic musical headspace that GN'R requires. I'm not saying a bass player doesn't need good chops to play these songs, but it's more of a full frontal attack, not necessarily a musical style that can be learned. I've seen bands cover our songs from time to time, but they always seem to be missing that guttural attack that the five of us original guys had in spades. I dropped my guitar strap a notch and started to let it fly.

"Rocket Queen"? Okay. I'm in!

This wasn't the absolute first time that Axl and I had communicated in all of that time. I had seen and even played with his band back in 2010, and I really listened to the live versions of their new songs from *Chinese Democracy* when I saw them play those shows with Loaded. It was totally weird to see "your" singer do his thing with a whole new set of musicians, but my gut reaction then was to pull for him. I realized then that all of my work on past resentments had actually paid off when it came to Axl. It was a great personal moment.

The word "resentment" itself is just a general term. If something happens in your life that you weren't onboard with or had no control over, have you ever asked yourself what your part in it might have been? Especially once that past event builds up in your head and becomes black and shitty?

I found some things in my past that I was blaming others for that I could have handled better. I think we have all looked at the bad things that have happened and, through the rear-view mirror of life, decided that it was all someone else's fault. Of course, when you look back with a bit more thoroughness, you realize that you, too, are in that rear-view mirror and that maybe, just maybe, you had something to do with the things you were pissed off or uneasy about. Resentments start to dwindle and fade, and oftentimes you can see the humor in your folly that is life.

I learned to deal with the me in my life through my Sensei Benny Urquidez and the brutal self-honesty that is Ukidokan martial arts. Without all of that, I'm not sure just where the hell I'd be now. But that is another story.

Over the last bunch of years, I've become pretty friendly with the guys in Axl's band. Guitarist Ron "Bumblefoot" Thal and I jammed together a few times, and he and drummer Frank Ferrer had come to my house in LA for a dinner party a few years earlier. Ron's wife, Jen, hit it off with Susan pretty well. It would be great to see Dizzy Reed again, and I had just spent the previous summer touring along with Richard Fortus and Dizzy's other band, the Dead Daisies. Richard Fortus is the father of two girls, like me, and we've spent hours discussing the ups and downs of raising young daughters. Guitarist DJ Ashba and I had hung out a couple times, and he plays in a band with one of my best buddies, Nikki Sixx. In short: if you've played music for as long as I have, the world gets pretty small and you get to know your contemporaries.

Even saying all of that, I still felt a bit weird about playing these old songs with a whole new set of people. The intentions were all good, and bassist Tommy Stinson (who I'd be, uh, replacing) was super thankful that I was able to do it. But, still, there is so much history there. How was this going to go down?

Simply put: it went just fine. All the guys in the band, Axl, and the crew bent over backward to make this thing go as smoothly as possible for me. We had band-only rehearsals eight hours a day for five days and got things cruising without any hiccups.

But I hadn't yet played a whole real show with Axl, and now in South America, where we had set attendance records in the '90s, how was this all going to go in front of an ultra-passionate crowd?

I flew down to Buenos Aires with Susan. The band had already played a handful of shows with Tommy on the tour before he went back to his Replacements commitment. I was announced just a couple days before my first gig with them in Buenos Aires, and the floodgates of speculation and murmurs of a full reunion started to percolate. I kept my head down and just practiced the set in my hotel room. I have a cool little headphone amp that plugs into my bass that I bring out in times like these. There is a direct in for an iPod or whatever so that I can play along to tunes, if necessary, and an out for headphones.

Susan wanted us to go sightseeing, but with GN'R being so beloved in these regions and people now knowing I was here, simple sightseeing became more interesting. She and I went to dinner one night with a few guys from the crew. The hotel we were staying at had a long walkway out, and there was security out front keeping a few hundred fans from banging on doors. But when Susan and I came out, the kids just went berserk. Okay. Done this drill before. With my sweet wife standing there in her hot-ass dinner dress, there was just no way I could take pictures with everyone. I never want to be rude or come off as some kind of a prick, but, hell, man, I was on a date!

Susan and I are full-time, all-of-the-time parents. We don't have some full-time nanny, and hence, when we get to do these little side trips, fancy times like these should be looked at as uninterruptable. I love to wine and dine her, and she likes to get dressed up here and there. Sorry, fans in front of the hotel. I'll get back to you all tomorrow. It was date time with this hot babe!

By the time we got to the restaurant, we were met full-on by the paparazzi. Really? Alright, so it was a rather popular place. They probably aren't here for us, right? Pop pop pop pop. Wrong. We walked into the restaurant fully blinded by the flashes from their cameras. A week earlier back home, I was cleaning up dog poo and trying to talk to my doctor's office about getting the blood-test results from my checkup for my pneumonia over the phone: "No. My name is Duff, not Doug. D-U-F-F McKagan, with an A-N at the end. No, not Jeff. Duff. Dusty? No, no, no. Duff! D-U-F-F!"

We had a really pleasant and fun dinner with our friends, and the Argentinian beef we ate was out of this world. So good, in fact, that I actually ate meat, not my usual deal.

The newspapers came out the next morning, and there we were. And by "we," I mean to say "they," as in Susan's breasts. Sure, our faces were sort of in the photo, too, but only for contrast. It was one of those pictures you see of the celebrities walking somewhere in a hurry with their heads down, because there are a hundred flashes going off in the dark. The headline read "Bras Optional!" Susan was wearing a simple little black dress (the chicks these days call them "LBDs"). In a city where the tango is king, and cleavage and high heels are the standard dress, we were left scratching our heads at the headline. I guess boobs sell papers, even in a place where boobs are already everywhere. Sue's boobs were a great hit in Buenos Aires apparently, and, personally, I agree. Susan's boobs are top shelf, and they should be celebrated. Again, I digress.

We had set up a little practice space in downtown Buenos Aires for us to go through the set one last time before gig day. I, for one, was going to have my shit tight before the rather large moment. The guys in the band had been doing this set for quite some time, and I didn't want to be the one to fuck anything up when showtime came.

Through all of this, though, I still hadn't seen Axl. Richard Fortus and I had become workout partners at the hotel gym. He and his girl, Kat, took Susan and me to a seriously nice dinner show with tango dancing on one of the nights leading up to the concert (at that tango show, I fantasized about secretly taking tango lessons, and then one night taking Susan out and sweeping her off her feet! But I digress . . . again.) Otherwise, it was just me in my room playing my bass: headphones on, iPhone cranked.

On gig day, I rode down to the venue with a few of the guys. I was as prepared as I could be for the music side of this thing. I was mentally ready, too. Using every bit of my martial arts training to calm myself and have a solid center, I felt prepared for the emotional part of playing songs that I had a part in writing years before and had been there for when we took these songs, as a band, to the rest of the world, city by city, inch by inch, giving my pound of flesh. My blood is in these songs, and, fucking hell, I almost didn't survive to see it all.

One of my nephews from Seattle had e-mailed me a couple days before the gig. Years before, he had done a high-school exchange program in Argentina and had remained close friends with a couple of the guys he went to school with. They had offered to fly him to Buenos Aires for the gig if he could get them into the show. It would be a sort of rock-and-roll high school reunion. But my nephew, J.T., wouldn't be landing until half an hour before the show started. That would give him a scant thirty minutes to navigate customs and get his ass through the heavy Buenos Aires traffic and to the show. I set up parking in the back of the venue for them and full carte blanche to the side of the stage. J.T.'s adventure to get to the show was a nice diversion for me. It gave me something else to think about. And it felt good to know that I'd have another family member there for me when I hit the stage.

Then it was showtime. I had warmed up on the bass, drunk my energy drink, and stretched, and I started the walk to the stage where I met up with my singer. We nodded and smiled at each other and suddenly everything fell into place. We walked out onto that stage together, and the people lost their minds.

I saw people crying. I assume it was because they never thought they'd ever see the two of us share a stage again. There were some moments that night when I could feel the intangible energy and spiritual presence that was the force of that original creation of Guns. That extra something popped in and out throughout that set, and it was simply amazing when it was happening. The chemistry of a band is something that just happens, and when that band formed back in 1985, we had found an exceptional chemistry with five guys coming from five completely different backgrounds.

This is not to say that Axl hadn't created a really good band himself. It was obvious to me that these guys were top players and have a cool swagger that is all their own. All of us came together so well that night. It was obvious that our rehearsing had paid off.

But that connection between Axl and me, the ease and grace and blood and that common experience of the extraordinary sonic boom that was the original Guns N' Roses, hadn't gone anywhere. In fact, with all of the sober and clean years in my back pocket, it seemed even stronger.

He and I rode back from the gig together that night with Susan and his manager. I think we were both relieved and happy to have gotten that first gig under our belts. I was tired from all of the brain work involved in mentally preparing for the shows. But we were into this thing now, and we had a day off before our next show in Asuncion, Paraguay.

I got a lot of e-mails and texts from friends back home that night and the next day. People were so curious to know how the show went. *Classic Rock* magazine asked if I'd write an article for their great monthly about my experience. I thought it was too fresh at that point to be as observational as I would have liked for a written piece. But it seemed like everyone was totally aware of what was going on down there.

Susan and I had one more day together. We got our picture taken with some street tango dancers, ate some local fare down in some discreet little marketplace, toured an old naval schooner, and then she was gone. It would just be me and the dudes for the rest of the tour.

I kind of get off on the unknowns in life these days. I used to be a bit scared about going around those dark corners. For a long while—before I got comfortable with myself—I would stay with the pack for fear of being exposed to surprises in life that I might not be comfortable with. I noticed along the way that confident people were the ones always taking chances and leading by example. I wanted some of that confidence. For a while, I didn't know how to find it.

Sensei Benny says confidence is knowing you can do something even before you've ever tried it.

Q: *Okay, Benny, so can you climb Mt. Everest?*
A: *Yes.*
Q: *But you've never even been to that altitude. And what about the cold and the physical beat down?*
A: *I will learn how to deal with the altitude. I will train. And I will learn how to climb. Yes, I can indeed climb Mt. Everest.*

And you know he could, if put to it.

This is an edict of Ukidokan martial arts that I tell myself every day. Now, in practice, I knew for sure I could not only do this thing with Axl and those guys in the band but I would excel at it. I had already tried it, and now I was getting more confident at every oncoming footfall.

Before our flight, there was a lobby call for 2 p.m. I waited in that lobby until about 2:30, and when no one showed up, I went to go see what the holdup was all about. Axl had been waiting for me in the car for thirty minutes. I absolutely hate being late. Shit! Sorry, dude. Apparently lobby call in their touring parlance means to meet in the vehicle at the appointed time. "Always waiting on Duff. . . . The story of my life," Axl mused out loud. Tongue? Check. Cheek? Check. If there was any tension in the air remaining after that first gig, this funny and self-aware comment thoroughly removed what remained.

(Side note: Guns N' Roses became known as not being quite, uh, punctual . . . and, well, it was never this author who caused our gig times to be pushed back . . . from what I remember, anyway.)

We had to fly into Paraguay through an awful rain and lightning storm. The small, powerful jet we were in could fly at very high elevations, so skirting above the storm I looked down at what seemed to be a hellish cauldron of nasty weather. But we weren't in it, and finally we were past it, and the storm became a mere passing sight.

When we landed in Paraguay, we went straight to the show—the Jockey Club, the same racetrack I had just played with Kings of Chaos. Riding in the car, we could see those ominous black clouds of rain and lightning heading our way. That innocent scenery we saw below us from

39,000 feet was now very real and heading straight toward the 15,000 people waiting at the show, not to mention all of the electrical gear on the stage already set up. BOOM. Lightning struck very close. BOOM BOOM. Two more, and right there at the venue!

Sound familiar?

We went inside to the dressing rooms that were basically big tents. The rain came and it was torrential. A promoter got on the PA system and instructed the crowd to take cover under the cement bleachers, and our gear got covered in massive tarps and big pieces of plastic. We waited, just hoping the storm would pass. Nothing we could do except sit and wait.

My always-too-active brain went straight to the scenario that we'd have to cancel the gig. By now, my understanding of these crazy weather patterns—and the fans' unmatched fortitude—should have put me at ease. But I couldn't help but worry that if we canceled, and the press in the States and UK got hold of the story (which they would in two seconds because of Twitter, etc.), that I'd get a million questions from all of those outside people about "GN'R CANCELS GIG IN PARAGUAY, BLAH, BLAH, BLAH." For certain, this rain and lightning was very real and pretty damn dangerous, and I was more worried about anyone getting hurt. But the reality of any given situation is the one thing that never gets portrayed correctly on Twitter or Facebook.

Just then the promoter came backstage. Apparently, the local weatherman predicted that the storm would pass over and abate in about fifteen minutes and would completely disappear. It did just that. The gear was uncovered, the fans returned to what had become an extremely muddy field, and we played for three hours. It was victorious for everyone.

Our next stop was La Paz, Bolivia, and because I have some experience with climbing mountains and the adverse effects of altitude, I was very aware of the fact that La Paz is perched at 13,000 feet. I know from experience that I start to teeter a bit mentally at 12,000 feet. Up there in La Paz, they recommend coca leaves and coca tea for the altitude, but this was just not an option for me and my pesky drug addiction thing.

There aren't that many shows up in La Paz. Many singers have a hard time performing in air that thin. As a result, the people of La Paz are absolutely starved for rock music. We landed at the airport above La Paz at about six in the morning, and the lack of oxygen was instantly apparent. We got in cars and wound all the way down to our hotel at 8,000 feet. Much better. I've been told I kind of seem drunk when I'm over 12,000 feet. I didn't want to give any of these guys the wrong impression. I was relieved to get to that lower altitude.

For Axl, this wasn't just some other gig: at this altitude, it was more like an athletic feat. But even then, vocal cords are tiny, tiny muscles. Thin, dry, and cold air can rip up a person's voice.

The night before the show, Axl and I took some time to hang out and chill, just the two of us. We talked about how the altitude was affecting us, and then the conversation morphed into a discussion of some things past. It was a natural conversation of things we did and didn't remember about our old band. It was a really good, cleansing experience that sort of gave me a second wind. Talking about things that may be lodged and stuck from the past, things that may still cause friction of sorts in your current life, always seems to have a lifting effect on us humans. I recommend it.

Axl killed it in the altitude that night. We played for two hours and forty-five minutes. Manly stuff.

The rest of those gigs went off without a hitch. There were moments on that stage when I was reminded of what remarkable songwriters we were together back when. Shit! We were only twenty, twenty-one years old when we wrote the lion's share of that stuff!

Playing "November Rain," standing next to Axl every night, I flashed back to us recording that song at A&M Studios in Hollywood in 1990 during the monthlong tracking of *Use Your Illusion.* We still had our game then, and though we were often in altered states, we completed the music for twenty-nine songs or so, and that was with a new, last-minute drummer, Matt Sorum. It was a sweet but chaotic time for the band. It was perhaps the last period that we could all attain the status of being somewhere close to getting on the same page. It was before we all got infected with conflict and before I was completely lost to the drugs and alcohol.

The tour was emotional and joyous but also somewhat bittersweet. I'd just been to South America. I'd just played the Jockey Club—I'd just played "Paradise City" in front of these fans, out to brave a rainstorm and a mountain of mud to see "their band" play at a racetrack. Barely six months ago, I'd been here with Slash, Matt, Gilby, and my brothers in Kings of Chaos, the balance of our *Use Your Illusion*–era Guns N' Roses. I wished they could have experienced this with us. And I hope that one day we can all get together for a handshake, a smile, and a good laugh at the whole thing.

It was so awesome to have that opportunity to sort out some things from my past. I realized when I was in it that not very many of us get that chance. It was right and righteous and completely grown-up and professional.

It made me a better man.

PRIORITIZE AND STRATEGIZE

HOME FOR A FEW DAYS DURING THE BEAUTIFUL Seattle summer, my hands got restless.

There never seems to be enough time in the Seattle summer. If you live in a milder climate, then you also have the luxury of having many more months of the year to do summer things. In Seattle, summer starts on July 5 and ends just after Labor Day. That means we only have about ten weeks to

1. have a proper summer where we spend time on the lake as a family,
2. see those outside summer concerts,
3. put on our own summer concerts,

4. wear our summer clothes that are about fifteen
   years old but look new because we barely wear
   them, and
5. fix all of the shit on the outside of our house.

That last one is critical. There are only a couple months
of better-than-average odds that you're not going to get
rained on. So everyone rushes to get their outdoor projects
done at the same time that they're rushing onto the lake to
soak up some rays and fire up the barbecue to cook up a few
precious outdoor meals.

Yes, there's always a rush of activity and fear of the oncoming rainy season.

But, with no rock shows or commitments coming up, I
cast my gaze at my house and asked, What can be fixed? As
I've said before, I like to do my own work around the house
as much as possible. And if I'm actually fixing a problem
rather than making one worse, all the better.

I noticed that the lawn pavers I put down (by hand!) out
back in 1999 were overgrown with grass. Job 1: Recut the
path. Heck, maybe then we'd USE that path (that I put
down by hand!). Job 2: Put in a new subelectrical fuse panel
for our basement. No problem. Job 3: It was definitely time
to clean out the garage. Happy to do it.

Then I took a look at my back deck.

The backside of my house in Seattle gets hit by the weather
twenty-four hours a day, seven days a week. Thankfully, the
house is made of brick, and for the most part the brick can

take the Pacific Northwest elements head-on. My wood deck and dock down on the lake, however, do not fare as well. Every three or four years, I have to strip and restain the entire surface. If I don't, it looks ghetto. Worse, the wood goes to rot if it's not taken care of properly. I took a look at my deck and dock and realized it was time. This was the project of the summer. This was a once-in-a-presidential-term project that I could check off my summer bucket list. I was thrilled.

Although I didn't have any gigs of my own coming up, Slash was going to be opening for Aerosmith at the Gorge in a few days. Now, listen: I always go and see Slash or any of my other friends when they come through Seattle, but the Gorge really isn't in Seattle. By any reasonable standard, it's not near Seattle at all. Most touring bands just see "Washington" on their tour itinerary, and rightfully assume that the Gorge must be near or in Seattle. The Gorge is in the center of the state, 130 miles from my house.

Slash e-mailed me and asked if I'd be in town and if I wanted "to get up and jam." I love to get up and jam whenever I can, but driving 130 miles each way to do it, not to mention that I really had to get after staining my deck, was going to make this simple jam something more than I could probably take on with Pacific Northwest rain imminent. I said I'd try to make it, and then thought about how to tell touring Slash that I'd have to miss his gig because my path needed mowing and my deck needed staining.

Funny enough, Matt Sorum was also in Seattle at the time for a wedding, and he and I were trying to figure out a day and time that we could go out to dinner with our wives. Matt has friends all over the world, so I wasn't surprised when he suggested we have dinner at his friend's house in a very exclusive area outside of town. And when I say "very exclusive," I am talking straight-up baller exclusive. Microsoft and Boeing president exclusive. "Who the hell do you know who lives there?!" I asked Matt.

Says Matt, "It's a friend of mine who owns fish-processing ships up in Alaska. He has done very well for himself and just loves rock music. I've jammed on his yacht before and at his house. He's got a helicopter in his backyard and a jet down at Boeing Field, but you would never know by meeting him. He's a cool dude, and he was in a Norwegian prog rock band in the '70s!"

Wow. OK. Nice guy. Into Norwegian prog rock. Sounds interesting. But I told Matt that I just couldn't invite Susan and myself to this guy's house for dinner and that we'd feel more than weird about it. Matt assured me that we were by all means invited and that this dude was a bass player and was happy I was coming over.

I wasn't surprised to hear that Matt had a friend in the fishing business who lived in Seattle. Fishing has always been a huge industry in my town. The lifeblood, really. Native Americans enjoyed as much fish as they liked for generations upon generations. In the late 1800s and early part of the 1900s, a huge Scandinavian diaspora filtered into the Puget Sound region to take advantage of the seemingly never-ending supply of fish. The supply, sadly, inevitably, did have an ending.

When the Puget Sound started to get fished out in the 1950s, the seafood industry began to turn its gaze north to Alaska. Seattle remains the business head of the massive salmon, crab, halibut, and whitefish industry. The world's fish sticks come from here. Think of just how many McDonald's are in the world, and multiply the amount of fish sandwiches they sell, and all of the frozen fish sticks there are in the countless freezer sections of the countless grocery stores in North America and Europe. The lion's share of this processed fish comes from Alaska via Seattle nowadays. It's a huge business.

I got directions to the house from my new friend, whom I'll just call Espen here (we're not quite to the "I'm gonna mention you by name in my memoir" kind of level yet, but I'm interested to see how it goes). Susan and I drove down a very long and beautiful driveway that led past a regular-sized and very nice house that I knew from Espen was the caretaker's house (as big as my house). The driveway went on, opening up to a massive mansion. This was some next-level shit.

Espen, along with Matt and his wife, Ace, came out to meet us, and Espen started to show us around. There was cool art and beautiful furniture, secret stairs to a studio, and more secret stairs to a gym. On the back lawn facing the sound, there was a jet helicopter. A jet fucking helicopter. The whole time Espen was showing us his house, it became apparent that he was as stoked as a kid about all of the cool shit. He wasn't born into it, that was evident. I needed some more info, and so I asked Espen his story.

In the early '70s, Espen was in a prog rock band in Norway. He and his wife were in their early twenties, and she got pregnant. His musical ambitions were suddenly stunted, as his wife brought up the fact that he needed to earn some dough now that they were going to have a child. Apparently, prog rock in the Norwegian language has a limited audience.

Espen started to fish on a small boat off the coast of Norway. Soon after, his brother joined him. It dawned on them that if they could buy their own little boat, they'd make a lot more money. They worked their asses off, saved, and finally bought a boat. Then a second one. Flash forward a few more years: Espen realized that if they had another boat to process the fish in, they could keep their fish fresher AND they could keep the fishing boats out at sea more often. The fish-processing boat thing caught on in a big way, and his reputation as a smart fisherman who produced came into play. His processing venture moved to Alaska, and the rest is history. But the point is, Espen worked his ass off, gambled, innovated, and it paid off. Helicopter, jet, yacht, and mansion paid off (oh, and Espen is a true Seattleite. He drives an electric car to and from work and loves the Seahawks!).

Humbled and amazed, I kept listening, and Espen treated us to a very nice salmon dinner. Espen's full-time chef is a funny guy—a culinary shitkicker, if you will. And I discovered it was he and his wife who lived in that nice house up the driveway. Matt and Ace had never really experienced Alaska salmon so fresh, and all in all it was a great evening that culminated in a big jam in Espen's studio. Susan and I were more than glad that we had done this night and made a new friend.

That was a Thursday night, and I knew it would be my last night of socializing before I tackled my deck on the last full weekend of sun we were going to get. The reality of making a trip out to the Gorge to jam with my bud was quickly becoming an unreality. On Friday, I went and got all of my supplies, bringing a little piece of the stained wood so that they could get a match at the paint store.

(Note: I've guessed at stain color in previous years, which apparently is not a good idea when you are a hue-challenged person like me. I started a stain job a few years back with the wrong color, a color I thought was "mission brown" but turned out to be some weird bright green that made my wife and daughters howl with laughter. That wasn't the "ooh-ahh" reaction I was hoping for.)

A couple hours later, I got a call from Espen. "Hey, Duff. Do you and Susan want to go over to see Slash and Aerosmith with me?" It was a kind offer, but I explained to Espen that I had stuff to do, and that there really wasn't time for me to make the drive. I didn't mention that it was a stain job, because at that point I really think I was the only one who thought it was a good idea that I do it myself instead of hiring someone. "No, man. We can take the jet. It's a twenty-minute flight each way. Just drive your car down to the field and park inside. You'll be back by midnight." Oh, right. The jet!

This I could do. If I was back by midnight, I could still get up at 7 a.m. and get to work on my chores. Besides, it was pretty generous of Espen to ask us along. I started to think of where the actual airfield was by the Gorge. Hmmm. I've played the Gorge a bunch of times, but I've never actually heard of anyone flying there. Espen's plan had one slight hiccup: he didn't have a way to get us from the airfield to the Gorge. The nearest airfield was about twenty miles away in a town called Quincy. There ain't no Uber, taxis, or car services in that part of the country. But, like I said, I'm very familiar with the Gorge and the logistics of getting to and playing at it. I may not be able to reciprocate my friend's flight with a turn on a private jet of my own, but I was sure I could handle getting us from the airfield to the show.

My friend Juan is the head of security for most of the big shows out there, so I gave him a call. "Hey, Juan. Can you get someone to pick us up?"

That's when things got interesting.

Juan wasn't actually working this particular gig, and, hence, he wouldn't be able to send someone from the site to get us. OK. No problem. I have friends at Live Nation, the owners of the Gorge. I called one, explained the situation and that I'd be sitting in with Slash and just needed to get from the airfield to the show. Did they have a runner who could come get us? Sorry, they said. No runners for the show.

OK. Hmmmm. I called Juan back. He works MOST of the shows. Do you know ANYONE who could come get us? Actually . . . he did. He knew a dude from Kirkland named Andrew who was going to the show. He was sure that Andrew wouldn't mind giving us a ride. Boom. We were set. I called Espen and told him I had a ride for us. "Splendid, Duff!" I felt like I'd just pulled some real rock-and-roll jiu-jitsu.

Susan and I drove south of downtown Seattle to Boeing Field. Wheels-up time on the plane was 5 p.m., and Susan and I get there at 4:45. We were led into a private and totally pimpin' airstrip parking area just next to a tricked-out jet, just fifteen minutes before takeoff. Our guest wasn't even there yet. At about 4:48, Susan and I start to wonder where Espen was. We asked the lady at the private air desk, and she explained that Espen was just circling above in his helicopter. Oh, yeah. The helicopter.

The flight over the Cascade Mountains was awe inspiring. I was beginning to be pretty glad that we were on the trip. Espen can actually fly the plane and does all of the time, but he wanted to drink some wine at the gig, so he hired a pilot to take care of us on the trip. Descending to the tiny airstrip, I could already see Andrew's white Jeep Cherokee parked outside the fence. We were all set.

Andrew turned out to be a really nice guy, a huge rock fan, and seemed to be happy to have a story to tell his friends back home. Off we went to the gig. I texted Slash that I was on my way, and he asked if I'd play "It's So Easy," a song I also sing. Cool. No prob.

As we drove, I asked Andrew where he was sitting during the show. "Oh," he explained, "I don't have tickets to the show. But Aerosmith is my favorite band. So I thought I'd come out and camp at the campground and see if I could find a way in." The guy had hit the jackpot. I thanked him for his help by securing full-access backstage passes.

Earlier that day, I had stripped my deck and dock back home, and I knew it would all be ready for my staining assault the next day. All was right in the world.

We got into the backstage area and got passes for Andrew and—critically—a parking spot for his Jeep. I told Andrew that he was my guest and so try to behave himself accordingly. He was a real gentleman and understood completely.

The gig went on without a hitch. I got to see my old pal play some scorching rock music and then got to see a great set from Aerosmith in that most beautiful amphitheater along the Columbia River. I have been friends with those guys since 1988, when GN'R did our dream tour with them just as *Appetite* was breaking out commercially. Hell, the Walking Papers had just gotten back from a European tour with these guys, so the whole thing was like going to see family.

As Aerosmith's set was getting going, Espen came up to me and invited Susan and me to his yacht in the San Juan Islands later that night. Steven Tyler was going to come on the plane with us, and Matt and his wife would meet us up there, too. We'd spend a few days just cruising the islands. I told Espen, though, that I really had to get back to Seattle because of some "stuff I had to do." It was tempting to spend a long weekend with my wife and friends on a private yacht in the San Juans. But in the back of my head I kept thinking, those boards in the backyard are not gonna stain themselves. They never do.

Let's see:

A. Go by private jet and helicopter to a yacht with one of my boyhood rock idols in tow and cruise the most beautiful part of the world, with a chef and full crew.
B. Get up at 7 a.m. and take care of my deck.

You know what happened. I've got to take care of my home and my family. Don't get me wrong, at any other point and time, I would have loved to go. I love the water. I love boats, and I love good company. But, again, the deck wasn't going to stain itself!

Then Espen asked another question, After the show, do you think Andrew could take us back to the plane?

Oh, right. Andrew! I looked around and found Andrew having the time of his life . . . and a few cocktails. "Andrew," I said. "Can you give us a ride back to the plane? We are bringing Steven Tyler with us now, too. Is there room? And, are you OK to drive?" I could tell Andrew was stunned: driving Steven Tyler in his car was going to be a story he could tell his grandkids! Andrew put down his drink, drank a pot of coffee, and sobered up.

After the show, we all piled into Andrew's Jeep, and he took us back to the plane. We all thanked him for his service and sent him on his way. I am convinced that my friends thought Andrew was a paid, professional driver. I never let on that he was a guy I had found through a friend who had just come out to the show and hit the rock-fan lottery. Andrew played his part like a pro.

When we got in the air, both Espen and Tyler were trying to convince me to come along with them. I started to think that I was a real buffoon, but the thought of one of my daughters, my wife, or a guest snagging a bare foot and getting a sliver on an eroding deck plank back home sealed the deal. "Nope, guys. I got stuff to do."

We dropped the guys off on Orcas Island, and Susan and I had the plane all to ourselves. The pilot said that he had enough gas in the jet to take us to Vegas if we wanted. No thanks, we had to go back home. At another point of my life, I would have done all of this stuff and more. But, I've got to say, I get a thrill out of the simple fact that I like to do this maintenance stuff at my house, and it is a major priority.

The next day, we woke up to a sunny, warm day in Seattle. Susan and I put on our work clothes and prepared for the job in front of us. The Seahawks were going to be playing a preseason game, and I'd be blasting the play-by-play on the dock.

I had to get in the water to stain the sides, and I was careful not to spill a drop into the lake. I looked up at the yard and saw my wife happily staining the deck. We had a blast and felt good knowing that our deck and dock would be secure for a few more years.

Matt sent us a bunch of pictures from the yacht. They all looked like they were having a great time, and I took a certain pride thinking about them enjoying our hidden treasures of the San Juan Islands. It was all good. I jammed with my buddy, I got to fly in a fancy jet, got to meet a new friend in Andrew, got to see Aerosmith, and I got to finish the daunting yet enjoyable task of doing my own work at home.

This, my friends, was a very good weekend.

EPILOGUE: NEVER QUIT DOING WHAT YOU LOVE

I FINISHED THIS BOOK ON A FLIGHT FROM LOS ANGELES to London, two days before Thanksgiving 2014. I was on my way to South Africa with the Kings of Chaos crew. This tour had an added perk: We were joined by ZZ Top's Billy Gibbons, Aerosmith's Steven Tyler, and the great Robin Zander from Cheap Trick. To call these men three of my heroes is an extreme understatement. You think Andrew from Kirkland was surprised to see Steven Tyler riding shotgun in his Jeep? Imagine what it feels like for him to shove a microphone in your face during "Toys in the Attic"!

When I was thirty, I asked a nurse to let me die. In a couple days, I'm going to play "Cheap Sunglasses" alongside the man who wrote it.

This tour—this year, the year that I turned fifty, that I've chronicled here—is the latest in a long line of surprises and blessings that I could not have comprehended in the lowest parts of my life. A time that coincided with the height of my band's fame.

When I got sober and completely flip-flopped my life, I thought my music career was over. I was still technically a member of Guns N' Roses, but I had somehow assumed with a dumb-ass certainty that one had to be inebriated to write songs and play onstage. I mean, really, who the hell does this rock thing without a little juice, a bump of coke, a glass of vodka, Valium, more cocaine, some needless boy/girl drama, whiskey, beer, opiates, Quaaludes, more vodka, and another snort of cocaine?

All of us reach tipping points in our lives when we cross over into a new chapter. It is what we do at these moments that dictates the "part deux" of our lives. For this there is no handbook. We can only hope that putting our heads down and forging ahead will get us through. Guys like me are too dull to do it any other way.

At the time, I didn't have the capacity to comprehend a future as a musician.

My mind was elsewhere.

Just focus on trying to not use for one more day. I'll think about all of this other stuff later. Get on the mountain bike and ride until you can't. Go to the dojo, and punch, kick, learn everything possible from Sensei Benny. Punch and kick and stretch until you can't anymore. Sweat this shit out. Learn. Try. Try fucking harder. Yes, Sensei. Yes, Sensei! Bow out, and go home and eat something good. Drink lots of water (water? this is a novel idea). Try to look at yourself in the mirror at home before bed. Did I do everything to the best of my ability today? Was I honest about every action and word spoken today? Really? Who you lyin' to? Yourself? That's pretty lame. I'll try harder tomorrow. Just don't use! Just. Don't. Use.

Music was put on the back burner. I couldn't surmise how I'd ever play live without my shield of inebriation. Little did I know at my crossroads then that I was so insanely dead wrong.

With ten months of sobriety under my belt, I was approached by one of my all-time heroes, Steve Jones of the Sex Pistols, to start a band with him, Matt Sorum, and Duran Duran's John Taylor. I hadn't played a live gig sober yet, and I wasn't sure how that was going to go.

My first gig with this new band, called Neurotic Outsiders, would be at the Viper Room in West Hollywood. I'd never played there before, and, to be honest, I was more nervous than ever. Would I have a panic attack onstage? Would I tense up and not be able to play? Would people stare at me and judge me? Would we be any good? But the thought of playing a small room after all of those massive GN'R shows was refreshing. As a musician, performing in small rooms really improves your playing. The sound systems are smaller and less forgiving than huge PAs. The audience is right there in your face and can watch your playing almost as if through a microscope. You have to be good.

Starting a new band this time was a bit easier. Shit, I was playing with Steve Jones, and he had a massive hand in the sound and songwriting of the Pistols. The songs he brought to the band from the get-go were stellar. I was also sort of living out a teenage punk-rock dream. I knew it was gonna be cool, no matter the size of rooms we played. Believing in something for the pureness of that something carries a lot of weight with a guy like me.

We rehearsed for two weeks leading up to the Viper Room gig, and driving down there from my house in Hollywood (that used to serve as my drug headquarters), I really felt that I was starting a new chapter in my life.

I wasn't sure how to get into the club. There was a line around the corner. Do I walk through the people in line? I hadn't been around this many folks since I'd been sober, and it felt as if everyone were staring at me. I felt a bit too aware, a bit too sober. It felt like four hundred sets of eyes were burrowing into the back of my head. I started to sweat. My breathing became shallow and fast. If I can't handle maneuvering through these people, how would I be able to play in front of them in a couple of hours?

Just then, Matt showed up and nonchalantly mingled with folks in line. I remember watching in awe as he made the whole thing look easy. "C'mon Duff! Follow me!" Matt said, sensing my unease. And that was it. I was in.

We walked down the small, dimly lit hallway that led to the stairs up to the main room. Once I saw our gear sitting there on the stage and our crew guys waiting for us to sound check, things became a bit more familiar.

I know how to do music. This is where I am supposed to be. Those people are here in anticipation of seeing this new band. They aren't staring at me in judgment. They are being polite and probably a bit shy. Right. Don't freak out, Duff.

This incident sticks in my mind as one of the illuminating moments in my life. Everyone who has lived and breathed on this planet has experienced a time of great change. That evening I realized that my brain was sending me all kinds of signals I wasn't used to receiving. My breathing quickened, and my thought processes went a bit awry as I wasn't used to any of this sober, social gig stuff.

The gear sitting on the stage snapped me out of it. The gear was a source of strength, proof that I was in a safe place, a situation I knew how to navigate. I learned from then on to envision a homing point (my gear on the stage, if you will) before I get into situations that might make me uncomfortable or ill at ease.

As I got adjusted to the dim light in the club, Sal, the club manager at the time, came up and told me that a rumor was going around outside in line, a rumor that I had gotten a facelift. A facelift?! Right. In the preceding year, I had lived a sober life and had sort of clung to the confines of my martial arts dojo and rode my mountain bike, and I'd dropped fifty pounds of booze and drug weight. More like a life-lift.

There had been no pictures of me taken during my gradual recovery, so it must have seemed like an instant change to some of the people standing outside. If I wasn't sure how to deal with social situations yet, it was apparent that some people weren't quite sure what to make of me either.

Steve and John Taylor were sitting backstage, and we all kind of hung out there as the doors opened. As I was warming up on my guitar, Jonesy asked how I was doing. "I'm good, Steve." He told me that he remembered his first sober gig and that this would probably be my clearest musical moment in years. "You are gonna play better than you have in a long time, mate." That was all I needed to hear.

The new band was really good, and it was a total blast, with a lot of humor among the four of us. Humor was something that had been missing in my life for some time, and I had forgotten how much I missed levity and bad jokes.

When we hit the stage, the place erupted and we laid into a perfectly kick-ass set of OG punk rock. Steve was anchored to my left, looking my way every now and then, checking and nodding his approval. John Taylor is a bad man on the bass, and it suddenly hit me that, right, Mr. Taylor and Duran Duran were a full-on movement in modern music. John is so mellow and low key that I guess he sort of disarms you to the fact that he is John FUCKING Taylor!

Matt was on the drums, and he too slowed my roll. I settled in with a group of guys who had my back. If this is what playing sober was gonna be like, I wanted a whole lot more of it.

When we came offstage after the set, I felt like it had been one of the biggest gigs I'd ever played. Sure, we were a new band, and it would be an uphill battle to take this thing to bigger places and all, but that was beside the point. It felt right and honest and had real fucking balls and intent. Those are the things that matter to guys like me.

I drove home that night by myself. No Hollywood party. No chicks. Certainly no drugs or booze. Getting into bed, I realized that I was more fulfilled musically right then than I had been in some time. The spark was back. I knew I would be able to carry on playing music without the aid of inebriates. I was ecstatic and relieved and really just plain happy. I watched a bit of Ken Burns's *Civil War* and fell off to a deep sleep.

The Neurotic Outsiders did not become my life. My family did.

At the time, I had a romantic notion of what I wanted in life. I guess I still do.

I was still aspiring to *It's a Wonderful Life,* the movie that had such a deep impact on me when I first saw it at age twelve. I wanted a family more than anything. I wanted that wife and those kids. I wanted to struggle and love and nurture and be Jimmy Stewart. I still use his role as George Bailey as a benchmark for how to be a dad and husband. My wife indulges me with one of those 1947 dramatic kisses and hugs once in a while (for some reason, though, when Susan is miffed at me, approaching her with one of these George Bailey just-got-my-life-back-isn't-life-grand? violent kisses and squeezes just doesn't seem to unmiff her all of the time, but sometimes it works).

Thanks to Steve Jones and company, I discovered that I could get onstage sober. But a woman? I wasn't quite ready for that stuff at all. I couldn't even fully look at myself in the mirror yet. How the hell could I be a Jimmy Stewart to my future Donna Reed, when I still had cysts of toxins popping up all over me as they were escaping their old home that was my body?

Forge ahead. Try harder. Do the thing that is directly in front of you, and don't think beyond that. Head down. Ears pinned back. Move in a direct line.

A friend of mine set me up on a blind-ish date. I saw a marvelous photo of this beautiful woman, as my friend dialed her number. I talked to her on the phone, and the rest is history. I found my Mary Bailey in Susan Holmes. She wanted the things I wanted. Kids. A chill life (she had just "done" seven years in the high-stress world of couture fashion modeling). And Susan cried the first time we watched *It's a Wonderful Life* together. Man . . . she gets me!

Flash forward a few years, and we are happily married with two sweet little daughters. We were married with our families as witnesses in a beautiful little ceremony in the backyard of the house I bought back in my hazy days. Even all fucked up, I had held on to fading hopes of one day having a family. And now it was really happening. All of it. Sober. Being a father. Trying to be a good husband. Trying to be a good student at Seattle University. Trying to start a new life.

But the music gene that I was born with—the recurring dreams I had as a child that I could never shake—was starting to demand attention. When you have this particular inside makeup, you don't feel completely whole unless you are getting music out. In my case, I wanted to create something new. I was playing guitar a bunch and even got a rehearsal space in Seattle so that I could jam with some friends. I created a Loaded record and played a couple shows with the band in Japan and around Seattle. I also played with some guys around town like Mark Lanegan and the Presidents of the United States of America.

Then in 2003 I got a call telling me that the great rock drummer Randy Castillo had passed away. Matt Sorum and Slash and I were asked if we'd play together again at a show in LA to benefit Randy's family. The three of us hadn't played together since the end of GN'R in 1993. I truly think that we'd been sort of avoiding the inevitable "Oh, right, so you are just gonna get a new singer then?" type of questions from the rock public at large, which we knew would happen if we played together. But we all quickly and unquestionably assented, as Randy was one of those guys who constantly bent over backwards for others his whole abbreviated life.

Playing together that night was a powerful thing.

But I was still in school, and Susan and I had three- and six-year-old girls at home in Seattle. When Matt and Slash and I decided to pursue what would become Velvet Revolver, there was no question that Susan and the girls would be there with me. We rented a small, three-bedroom duplex in Hollywood as the band began its ten-month foray into writing songs and finding a singer.

As that band progressed and toured, my family got to come on the road with me quite a bit. I much preferred it that way and knew I was fortunate to be able to do it. VR was playing big enough places that the economics of the thing allowed for me to have the best of both worlds.

I found that it wasn't a "this or that" situation. I could be an active musician and a father and a husband and a bandmate. I could do the thing that I loved and support the family I'd always wanted.

I was gaining confidence in life as a whole. I started to write for *Playboy* and *Seattle Weekly* and ESPN, and I found that writing soothed some parts of those creative spasms that I will continue to maintain until the day I'm gone.

But, until then, I wanna use myself up. I want to live this life to its fullest. I want to see all that I can see and love all that I can possibly love. Those crossroads that I experienced were necessary turning points in my life. They allowed me to know now that when my life comes to its end point, I will slide headlong into my grave, exclaiming "Wow! What a ride!"

At least that's what I'm working on.

ACKNOWLEDGMENTS

In no particular order, I'd like to thank the following people and components that helped me get to the point that I could actually write this book.

Of course, my wife, Susan Holmes McKagan, and our daughters, Grace and Mae, come first.

I'd like to thank Barrett Martin, Ben Anderson, and Jeff Angell of the Walking Papers.

Our crew, Paul Spencer, Rob Jones, and Jay Smith.

The Loaded guys: Mike Squires, Jeff Rouse, and Burke Thomas.

My trusty editor and collaborator of seven years, Mr. Chris Kornelis.

Tim Mohr.

Ben Schafer and all at Da Capo Press.

My book agent, Dan Mandel.

I'd also like to thank Benny and Sara Urquidez, coffee, French presses, Advil, Alka-Seltzer Plus Cold, prednisone, antibiotics, Dr. Knapp, Dr. Ballin, Everlast boxing gloves, jump ropes, the CEO of BlackBerry, gyms around the world, Tim Medvetz, Mt. Rainier,

Mt. Baldy, stairs, big-ass Nalgene water bottles, energy drinks of all brands, shapes, and sizes, Axl Rose, Izzy Stradlin, Slash, Matt Sorum, Gilby Clarke, Steven Adler, McBob, Steven Tyler, Robin Zander, Billy Gibbons, Joe Elliott, Glenn Hughes, Dave Grohl, Corey Taylor, Ed Roland, Ron Mesh, Billy Duffy, Nikki Sixx, my travel agent Pat Rainer, United Airlines, Alaska Airlines, Easy (sleazy) Jet, British Airways, Lufthansa, American Airlines, TAM Airlines, Czech Airlines (even though you lost my bags), South African Air, Quantas, Air Emirates, Turkish Airways, Southwest Airlines, Delta Airlines, SAS Airlines, Jay Smith's Van Rentals, Motel 6, Travelodge, St. Regis Hotel, Amsterdam Youth Hostel, Super 8 Motel, the Four Seasons Hotel, the Ritz Hotels, the bunkhouse in the back of that club in Cologne, Germany, Chrome Hearts, my sleeping bag, Ben Gibbard, Nick and Kate Harmer, sliced meat, sliced cheese, protein bars, Plant Fusion protein powder (no gas!), Auto Grille truck stops, Flying J truck stops, almonds, Aerosmith, Sean Kinney, Jerry Cantrell and all of Alice in Chains, Billy Ray Cyrus, Ghost, Bon Jovi, Death Cab for Cutie, Billy Idol, Randy Blythe, Scott Uchida, the Pink Slips, Whitesnake, Slayer, Biffy Clyro, Alter Bridge, that shitty orange tour bus in Europe, our American bus driver Chris, Mac computers, Lasik eye surgery, Marshawn Lynch, Richard Sherman, Kam Chancellor, Russell Wilson and all of the Seattle Seahawks!, Andrew from Kirkland, Core Power Yoga, PUSH Fitness and Chad Landers, Oxford University Sport, Leicester University Fitness Centre, Washington Athletic Club, my own damn bed, Kindle, Fender guitars and amplification, Buckley and Twirlz, "healthy-weight" dog food, Woolite travel-size clothing detergent for your sink, Old Spice deodorant, Gucci men's perfume stuff, vitamin C, zinc, vitamin D, clean socks, dirty magazines, good books, great music, and all of the fine people that I have met on my travels.

About the Author

DUFF MCKAGAN is a writer, musician, and serial entrepreneur. He has founded or cofounded numerous internationally recognized corporations, including Guns N' Roses, Velvet Revolver, and Meridian Rock, a wealth management firm. He has written regular columns for ESPN.com, SeattleWeekly.com, and Playboy.com. His first book, *It's So Easy (and other lies)*, was a *New York Times* best seller. He lives in Seattle with his wife, daughters, and dogs.

About the Collaborator

CHRIS KORNELIS edited Duff's *Seattle Weekly* column for five years. He is a regular contributor to the *Wall Street Journal* and is writing a book about the first forty weeks of fatherhood. He lives in a reasonably priced real estate market outside Seattle with his wife, kids, and cats.

INDEX